I0482700

This Page left blank Intentionally

Table of Contents

I. PROJECT LIST BY SECTOR

Country	Projects	ADB Assistance
Note: Click on the project title for full details.		
AGRICULTURE and NATURAL RESOURCES SECTOR		
Pakistan	Jalalpur Irrigation Project	Approved TA
Bangladesh	Coastal Towns Infrastructure Improvement Project	Proposed loan
Cambodia	Climate Resilient Rice Commercialization Sector Development Program	Approved loan
China	Jiangxi Zhelin Lake Water Resources Integrated Utilization Project	Proposed loan
China	Guangdong Chaonan Water Resources Development and Protection Demonstration Project	Proposed loan
Philippines	Comprehensive Development for the Agusan River Basin	Proposed loan
EDUCATION SECTOR		
Bangladesh	Skills for Employment	Proposed loan
China	Guangxi Nanning Vocational Education Development	Proposed loan
China	Hunan Technical and Vocational Education and Training Demonstration Project	Approved loan
China	Gansu Jinta Concentrated Solar Power Project	Proposed Loan
India	Himachal Pradesh Clean Energy Transmission Investment Program - Tranche 2	Proposed Loan
Nepal	Skills Development Project	Proposed loan
Sri Lanka	Education Sector Development Program	Approved Loan
Tajikistan	Access to Green Finance Project	Approved TA
Philippines	Education Improvement Sector Development Program	Proposed TA
ENERGY SECTOR		
Afghanistan	Gas Development Master Plan	Approved TA
Azerbaijan	Renewable Energy Development (Biomass Cogeneration) Project	Proposed loan
Bangladesh	Regional Power Generation and Transmission Project (formerly Energy Efficiency Improvement Project II)	Proposed loan
Bangladesh	Regional Power Generation and Transmission Project (formerly Energy Efficiency Improvement II)	Proposed TA
Bhutan	Green Power Development Project II	Proposed loan
China	Qinghai Delinha Concentrated Solar Energy Plant Project	Proposed loan
Nepal	Rural Electrification through Renewable Energy	Proposed loan
Pakistan	Power Sector Rehabilitation Project	Proposed loan
Sri Lanka	Green Power Development and Energy Efficiency Improvement Investment Program	Approved TA
Timor-Leste	District Capital Power Distribution Project	Proposed grant
Tonga	Outer Island Renewable Energy Project	Approved grant
Turkmenistan	Zerger Regional Power Generation Project	Proposed loan
Uzbekistan	Takhiatash Power Plant Efficiency Improvement Project	Proposed loan
ENVIRONMENT SECTOR		
Bangladesh	Khilkhet Water Treatment Plant Project	Proposed loan
Bangladesh	Khilkhet Water Treatment Plant Project	Proposed loan
Bangladesh	Coastal Towns Infrastructure Improvement Project	Proposed loan
Cambodia	Urban Water Supply and Sanitation (formerly Rural Water Supply and Sanitation Project III)	Proposed loan
China	Yunnan Chuxiong Urban Environment Improvement Project	Proposed loan
China	Anhui Huainan Urban Water Systems Integrated Rehabilitation Project	Proposed loan
China	Hubei Huanggang Integrated Urban Environment Improvement Project	Proposed loan

Country	Projects	ADB Assistanc
Note: Click on the project title for full details.		
	ENVIRONMENT SECTOR	
China	Guangxi Baise Integrated Urban Environment Rehabilitation	Proposed loa
China	Gansu Jiuquan Integrated Urban Environment Improvement Project	Approved Loa
Philippines	Solid Waste Management Sector Project	Proposed loa
Philippines	Urban Water Supply and Sanitation Project	Proposed loa
Philippines	Angat Water Transmission Improvement Project	Proposed loa
Philippines	Water District Development Sector Project – Loan	Approved loa
Philippines	The Procter & Gamble Company Waste to Worth Project	Approved TA
Philippines	Climate Resilience and Green Growth in Critical Watersheds	Proposed TA
Philippines	Water District Development Sector Project - TA	Proposed TA
	HEALTH SECTOR	
Myanmar	GMS Capacity Building for HIV/AIDs Project (Strengthened National Response to HIV and AIDS in Myanmar)	Proposed Grant
	INDUSTRY, FINANCE, and OTHER SECTORS	
Bangladesh	Third Urban Governance and Infrastructure Improvement Project - Project Design Advance	Proposed loa
Bangladesh	Third Urban Governance and Infrastructure Improvement (Sector) Project	Proposed loa
Bangladesh	Second Public-Private Infrastructure Development Facility (PPIDF II)	Proposed loa
Cambodia	Third Financial Sector Program - Subprogram 2	Approved loa
Cambodia	Public-Private Partnership Development Project	Proposed loa
China	Henan Value Chain and Products Safety Demonstration Project	Proposed loa
China	Chongqing Urban-Rural Infrastructure Development Demonstration II Project	Proposed loa
China	Xinjiang Tacheng Border Cities and Counties Development Project	Proposed loa
India	Meghalaya Public Management Reform Program	Proposed loa
India	Catalyzing Sustainable Finance Facility	Proposed loa
India	Punjab Development Finance Program	Proposed loa
India	Supporting Human Capital Development in Meghalaya	Proposed loa
Pakistan	Punjab Millennium Development Goals Program - Subprogram 3	Proposed loa
Philippines	Support for Data Management for Performance Reporting and Assessment	Approved TA
Philippines	Supporting Capacity Development for the Bureau of Internal Revenue (BIR)	Proposed TA
Philippines	Community-Driven Development Support Project	Proposed loa
Philippines	PFM 3 [previously Governance and Public Financial Management Phase I (Cluster TA)]	Proposed TA
Philippines	Second Road Improvement & Institutional Development Project	Proposed TA
Regional	Midterm Review of the Republic of Korea e-Asia and Knowledge Partnership Fund	Approved TA
Regional	Greater Mekong Subregion: Livelihood Support for Corridor Towns	Approved gra
Regional	Provision of Knowledge Products and Services to DMCs through Systematic Knowledge Sharing	Approved TA
Regional	Greater Mekong Subregion Phnom Penh Plan for Development Management Phase V	Approved TA
Vietnam	Strengthening Microfinance Sector Operations and Supervision	Approved TA
Vietnam	Strengthening Support for State-Owned Enterprise Reform and Corporate Governance Facilitation Program	Approved TA
	TRANSPORTATION and COMMUNICATIONS SECTOR	
Afghanistan	Rehabilitation of Bamian-Yakawlang Road	Approved Gra
Bangladesh	South Asia Subregional Economic Cooperation Road Connectivity Project	Approved loar
Bangladesh	Subregional Railway Connectivity: Akhaura-Laksam Double Track Project	Proposed loar
Bangladesh	Subregional Railway Connectivity: Akhaura-Laksam Double Track Project	Proposed loar
Bhutan	SASEC Road Connectivity Project (formerly Road Network Project II (Additional Financing))	Proposed loar
China	Jiangxi Ji'an Sustainable Urban Transport Project	Proposed loar
China	Yuxi-Mohan Subregional Railway Link Project	Proposed loar
China	Yunnan Sustainable Road Maintenance Project	Proposed loar

Country	Projects	ADB Assistance
Note: Click on the project title for full details.		
	TRANSPORTATION and COMMUNICATIONS SECTOR	
China	Yunnan Pu'er Regional Integrated Road Network Development Project	Proposed loan
China	Anhui Intermodal Sustainable Transport Development Project	Proposed loan
China	Inner Mongolia Road Development Project	Proposed loan
India	West Bengal North-South Corridor Project (formerly West Bengal Haldia Port Connectivity Project)	Proposed loan
Kyrgyz	CAREC Corridor 3 (Bishkek-Osh Road) Improvement Project, Phase 4	Proposed loan
Myanmar	Design of e-Governance Master Plan and Review of Information and Communication Technology Capacity in Academic Institutions	Approved TA
Nepal	Bagmati River Basin Improvement Project	Proposed loan
Philippines	Second Road Improvement & Institutional Development Project	Proposed TA
	URBAN DEVELOPMENT SECTOR	
China	Jilin Urban Services Improvement Project	Proposed loan
China	Hubei-Yichang Sustainable Urban Transport Project	Proposed loan
China	Xinjiang Integrated Urban Development	Proposed loan

II. LOAN

NOTE: Please click on the project title to access full project information.

AZERBAIJAN

Renewable Energy Development (Biomass Cogeneration) Project

Project No.	:	**47008-002 (Proposed)**
Amount (US $ million)	:	**40**
Executing Agencies	:	**State Agency on Alternative & Renewable Energy Source**
Sector	:	**Energy**

Status: Management Review Meeting scheduled in June 6, 2014

Description: The Project aims to promote renewable energy development in Azerbaijan through developing two pilot renewable energy projects (biomass cogeneration) with a total installed capacity of 16 megawatt (MW) for efficient electricity and heating supply in Oghuz and Agjabedi regions. The project impact will be efficient and sustainable renewable energy development in Azerbaijan. The expected project outcome will be increased Renewable Energy share in power generation by demonstrating the viability of biomass cogeneration plants and heating supply systems in Oghuz and Agjabedi regions. The project outputs will consist: (i) construction of two biomass cogeneration plants in Oghuz and Agjabedi regions; (ii) construction of heating supply systems in Oghuz and Agjabedi regions; and (iii) project management and supervision, including consultancy services for project supervision, safeguards compliance, reporting, and capacity building for the executing agency.

Business Opportunities:

- Consulting Services: To assist the EA in implementation, a supervision consulting firm will be recruited using the quality- and cost-based selection (QCBS) method (90:10), in accordance with ADB's Guidelines on the Use of Consultants (2010, as amended from time to time).

- Procurement: The Project will be implemented by turnkey contractors. The indicative procurement methods will be international competitive bidding (ICB), in accordance with ADB's Procurement Guidelines (2010, as amended from time to time).

Responsible ADB Officer: Tianhua Luo (E-mail: tluo@adb.org)
Central and West Asia Department
Energy Division, CWRD

BANGLADESH

A. Subregional Railway Connectivity: Akhaura-Laksam Double Track Project

Project No.	:	46168-001 (Proposed)
Amount (US $ million)	:	200
Executing Agencies	:	Bangladesh Railway (BR)
Sector	:	Transport and ICT

Status: Proposed; management review meeting scheduled on September 30, 2013

Description: The main objective of the project is to construct the second track between Laksam and Akhaura to complete the seamless double track railway line in the Dhaka-Chittagong corridor and to upgrade the existing track according to the requirements of the Trans Asian Railway network. Dhaka and Chittagong are the two major metropolitan areas of Bangladesh. Dhaka is the main commercial and administrative center of the country; Chittagong is the primary seaport, accounting for about 90% of imports and exports. More than a quarter of Bangladesh's population of 142 million lives in the Dhaka-Chittagong corridor. The government's Sixth Five-Year Plan, 2011-2015 assigns the highest priority to increasing the capacity of the Dhaka-Chittagong corridor by completing double tracking on the entire corridor, which is important to increase the market share of the railway. Enhancing the capacity of the Laksam-Akhaura section will also allow operating additional trains for subregional trade through Chittagong Port with Bhutan, India and Nepal; the project is part of the Trans Asian Railway (TAR) network.

Impact: Efficient and safe transport system in the Dhaka-Chittagong corridor

Outcome: Improved railway transport capacity in the DhakaChittagong corridors

Outputs:
1. Laksam-Akhaura Double Track completed
2. Project management capacity enhanced

Business Opportunities
- Consulting Services: To be determined

- Procurement Notices: To be determined

Responsible ADB Officer: Markus Roesner (E-mail: mroesner@adb.org)
South Asia Department
Transport and Communications Division, SARD

B. Dhaka Environmentally Sustainable Water Supply Project

Project No.   :   42173-013 (Proposed)
Amount (US $ million) :   250
Executing Agencies :   Ministry of Finance
Sector   :   Water Supply and Sanitation

Status: Proposed; management review meeting scheduled on June 3, 2013

Description: The project will provide more reliable and sustainable water supply in Dhaka by developing a new surface water source for supply augmentation. It will prepare priority investments in wastewater management system development ready for bidding to cope with increased volume of wastewater, and advance strengthening of the capacity of Dhaka Water Supply and Sewerage Authority (DWASA) and sector policy reform, building on the achievements under the ongoing ADB-financed sector development program.

Project Rationale and Linkage to Country/Regional Strategy: The government has set a target of providing all urban areas with safe water coverage and full sanitation by 2015. However, achieving this target remains a major challenge for the country, with population growth in urban areas doubling that of national average. This is no exception for Dhaka, capital of Bangladesh. It had a population of 14.6 million in 2010, the 9th largest in the world, and it is projected to be the 5th largest by 2025 with a population of 20.9 million. DWASA currently provides water supply to the population of about 10.3 million in about 70% of the Dhaka Metropolitan Area, but is unable to provide sufficient quality and quantity of water to its beneficiaries despite significant improvements. Moreover, as it heavily relies on the groundwater as source of water supply (about 90%), the groundwater table is falling by 2-3 meters per year. According to an estimate, about 50% of deep tube wells in the upper aquifer will become inoperative by 2015, reducing significantly the groundwater production. While further study of sustainable groundwater extraction in Dhaka is warranted, current extraction of about 1,900 million liters per day (MLD) needs to be reduced to about 900 MLD, including new aquifer development, under a realistic scenario.

Impact: Improved access to water supply services in Dhaka

Outcome: More reliable and sustainable water supply in Dhaka.

Outputs:
1. Program implemented for surface water supply augmentation.
2. Priority investments for wastewater management system prepared.
3. Project management and administration supported.

Business Opportunities
   ▪   Consulting Services: To be determined

   ▪   Procurement: To be determined

Responsible ADB Officer: Norio Saito (E-mail: nsaito@adb.org)
                                    South Asia Department
                                    Urban Development and Water Division, SARD

C. Third Urban Governance and Infrastructure Improvement Project - Project Design Advance

Project No.   :   39295-034 (Proposed)
Amount (US $ million) :   5
Sector   :   **Multisector**

Project details yet to be provided

Status: Proposed; management review meeting scheduled on August 19, 2013

Responsible ADB Officer: Norio Saito (E-mail: nsaito@adb.org)
South Asia Department
Urban Development and Water Division, SARD

D. Regional Power Generation and Transmission Project (formerly Energy Efficiency Improvement Project II)

Project No.   :   41160-013 (Proposed)
Amount (US $ million) :   260
Sector   :   **Energy**

Project details yet to be determined

Status: Proposed; management review meeting scheduled on August 18, 2013

Responsible ADB Officer: Priyantha D.C. Wijayatunga (E-mail: pwijayatunga@adb.org)
South Asia Department
Energy Division, SARD

E. Coastal Towns Infrastructure Improvement Project

Project No.   :   44212-013 (Proposed)
Amount (US $ million) :   52
Executing Agencies   :   **Local Government Engineering Department**
Sector   :   **Water Supply and Sanitation**

Status: Proposed; management review meeting scheduled on September 23, 2013

Description: The project takes a holistic and integrated approach to urban environmental improvement in vulnerable coastal towns of Bangladesh, which suffers deficits in basic urban services and is severely at risk to the impacts of climate change. It will provide climate resilient municipal infrastructure, including water supply, sanitation, drainage, flood protection, urban roads, and solid waste management facilities, and will strengthen institutional capacity and local governance for operating, maintaining, and expanding access to such services. The project will also mainstream climate resilience into urban planning. The Local Government Engineering Department (LGED), with extensive experience in managing Asian Development Bank (ADB) and other donor supported urban projects, will be the Executing Agency for the Project. Climate change and variability are critical development issues for Bangladesh, particularly in its low lying coastal areas naturally exposed to sea level rise, storm surges, and more frequent and intense storm events. The government, in its Sixth Five-Year Plan, FY2011 FY2015, has targeted assistance to vulnerable coastal populations with improvements in climate resilient water supply, sanitation, drainage, and flood protection infrastructure. The project was prioritized in the government s 2010 Strategic Program for Climate Resilience (SPCR), prepared under the Pilot Program for Climate Resilience (PPCR). , As a key component of the SPCR, the project is eligible for financing from the Strategic Climate Fund (SCF) within the multi-donor coordinated Climate Investment Funds (CIF) as a pilot project for demonstrating ways to mainstream climate resilience into development. The coastal areas of Bangladesh consist of three distinct regions, namely the western, central and eastern zones comprising 19 districts. The coastal towns, with population of around 7 million, include both smaller pourashavas (secondary towns) and larger cities such as Khulna, Chittagong, and Barisal. , Infrastructure is currently inadequate in these areas as they are either damaged by natural disasters or otherwise no longer functioning effectively. Weak local governance and municipal management coupled with high poverty incidence, and remote locations, create persistent development challenges to these areas. Climate change, variability, and natural disasters further aggravate development in coastal towns, with disproportionate impacts to women and the poor. The increased incidence of drought and saline intrusion (from sea level rise and storm surges) into groundwater, coupled with high non-revenue water, is posing serious risks to drinking water supplies, requiring the potential for developing new, but costlier, water supply sources located at far distances. Poor access to sanitation in coastal towns is also posing serious public and environmental health risks (Bangladesh is currently behind in achieving its MDG Target 10 indicators for urban sanitation). Drainage systems are underdeveloped and poorly maintained, and would be made further obsolete under more intense and frequent storm events. Given this scenario, future investments in urban infrastructure need to be climate-resilient to manage the long-term costs of investments, and to ensure that such investments deliver their intended benefits.

Project Rationale and Linkage to Country/Regional Strategy: The project will take a participatory approach to address the social, environmental, and institutional constraints to inclusive development in coastal towns, and will serve to pilot new approaches in climate adaption to be scaled up under future investments. It will reflect lessons learned from the first and second Urban Governance and Infrastructure Improvement (Sector) Projects (UGIIP), TA 7197 Strengthening Resilience of the Water Sector in Khulna to Climate Change, TA 7848 Climate Change Capacity Building and Knowledge Management, and recommendations from the ongoing CDTA 7890 Strengthening the Resilience of the Urban Water Supply, Drainage, and Sanitation to Climate Change in Coastal Towns related to the location of water-intake works, the appropriate design of drainage systems, and urban wastewater discharge. The project will also closely coordinate with the World Bank and other donors working in the urban sector to avoid duplication and ensure complementarities. ADB's Country Operations Business Plan (2012 2014) lists the Coastal Towns Infrastructure Improvement Project for implementation in 2013. The project is consistent with ADB's Bangladesh Country Partnership Strategy (2011-2015) which targets assistance to vulnerable coastal areas in adapting to the risks of climate change, as well as ADB s urban and water operational plans.

Impact: Improved health in coastal town populations

Outcome: Improved access to more reliable and climate-resilient municipal services in coastal towns

Outputs:
1. Improved municipal infrastructure with climate-resilient design in coastal towns
2. Strengthened local governance and capacity for sustainable service delivery and urban planning
3. Awareness raising and behavioral change programs implemented
4. Project management and administration support established

Business Opportunities
- *Consulting Services*: A firm and individual consultants will be recruited in accordance with ADB s Guidelines on the Use of Consultants (2010, as amended from time to time). Consulting firms will

be recruited using Quality and Cost-Based Selection (QCBS) method with a quality:cost ratio of 80:20.

- *Procurement*: All procurement to be financed under the project will be carried out in accordance with ADB's Procurement Guidelines (2010, as amended from time to time).

Responsible ADB Officer: Ron H. Slangen (E-mail: rslangen@adb.org)
South Asia Department
Urban Development and Water Division, SARD

F. South Asia Subregional Economic Cooperation Road Connectivity Project

Loan No.   :   **2949; 8263**
TA No.   :   **8221**
Project No.   :   **40540-014**
Amount (US $ million) :   **198**
Executing Agencies   :   **Roads and Highways Department**
                              Bangladesh Land Port Authority

Sector   :   **Transport and ICT**

Status: Board approved on November 22, 2012

Description: The project will: (i) upgrade about 110 kilometers (km) of Dhaka-Northwest corridor by 4-laning of the Joydebpur-Chandra-Tangail-Hatikamrul Road and (ii) improve 2 land ports at Benapole and Burimari. This trunk road section forms part of a major international road corridor. The project will also strengthen the capacity of the road sector. By increasing road capacity of a major international trade corridor and enhancing land port capacity, the project will not only boost the national economy but also facilitate subregional cooperation and increase trades.

Business Opportunities:
- *Consulting Services*: An estimated 2,710 person-months (249 international, 2,461 national) of consulting services are required to: (i) facilitate project management and implementation for LPA and RHD, and (ii) enhance operational efficiency of LPA. Consulting firms will be engaged using the quality- and cost-based selection (QCBS) method with a quality:cost ratio of 90:10. A higher quality ratio is adopted because the task involves a certain level of innovativeness to coordinate with LPA and RHD, and to mobilize and manage several teams at the same time. To engage quality consultants in a timely manner, ADB and the government have agreed that ADB carry out consultant selection on behalf of the government. The government will retain its authority for contract negotiation and contract signing. The proposed TA will undertake 3 major components: (i) maintenance scheme for roads and bridges, (ii) overloading control scheme, and (iii) RHD modernization, covering institutional changes and streamlining business processes. As part of the capacity development for procurement processes, the TA will also provide for a procurement review to be undertaken for the proposed project. It is proposed that ADB will finance $1,500,000 equivalent, on a grant basis from a trust fund.

- *Procurement*: Procurement activities will be the responsibility of the Project Directors, who will be supported by the consultants under TA loan 2688 and the PIC. ADB engaged an international consultant during procurement processes for probity. ADB will closely monitor all procurement and implementation activities. Contracts for civil works and goods will comprise about 7 international competitive bidding (ICB) packages. Contract packages for equipment under RHD institutional development will be based on required technical features and timing of procurement.

Packages will be identified during implementation by consultants engaged under technical assistance.

Responsible ADB Officer: Hiroaki Yamaguchi (E-mail: hyamaguchi@adb.org)
South Asia Department
Transport and Communications Division, SARD

G. Subregional Railway Connectivity: Akhaura-Laksam Double Track Project

Project No.   :   46168-001 (Proposed)
Amount (US $ million) :   200
Executing Agencies   :   Bangladesh Railway (BR)
Sector   :   Transport/ICT

Status: Management review meeting scheduled on September 30, 2013

Description: The main objective of the project is to construct the second track between Laksam and Akhaura to complete the seamless double track railway line in the Dhaka-Chittagong corridor and to upgrade the existing track according to the requirements of the Trans Asian Railway network. Dhaka and Chittagong are the two major metropolitan areas of Bangladesh. Dhaka is the main commercial and administrative center of the country; Chittagong is the primary seaport, accounting for about 90% of imports and exports. More than a quarter of Bangladesh's population of 142 million lives in the Dhaka-Chittagong corridor. The government's Sixth Five-Year Plan, 2011-2015 assigns the highest priority to increasing the capacity of the Dhaka-Chittagong corridor by completing double tracking on the entire corridor, which is important to increase the market share of the railway. Enhancing the capacity of the Laksam-Akhaura section will also allow operating additional trains for subregional trade through Chittagong Port with Bhutan, India and Nepal; the project is part of the Trans Asian Railway (TAR) network.

Impact: Efficient and safe transport system in the Dhaka-Chittagong corridor

Outcome: Improved railway transport capacity in the Dhaka Chittagong corridors

Outputs:
1. Laksam-Akhaura Double Track completed
2. Project management capacity enhanced

Business Opportunities:
- Consulting Services: To be determined

- Procurement Notices: To be determined

Responsible ADB Officer: Markus Roesner (E-mail: mroesner@adb.org)
South Asia Department
Transport and Communications Division, SARD

H. Third Urban Governance and Infrastructure Improvement (Sector) Project

Project No.   :   39295-013 (Proposed)
Amount (US $ million) :   150
Executing Agencies   :   **Department of Public Health Engineering**
                                          Local Government Engineering Department

Sector   :   **Mutisector**

Status: Fact-finding scheduled on December 2 – 14, 2013

Description: The project will strengthen urban governance and improve urban infrastructure and service delivery in select pourashavas (municipalities) in Bangladesh. Building upon the successful implementation of earlier phases, the project adopts performance-based allocation of investment funds to municipalities as an incentive mechanism for governance reform. Physical investments in water supply and sanitation, drainage, roads, solid waste management, and other municipal facilities will be made through an integrated approach to improve the urban environment and foster economic growth.

Project Rationale and Linkage to Country/Regional Strategy: Pourashavas are struggling to provide their citizens with key services including drinking water supply and sanitation, roads, solid waste management, drainage systems, and other municipal services such as kitchen markets, street lights, and bus terminals. Although coverage in drinking water supply reached 85% in urban areas in 2010 (81% for the whole country), access to piped water supply in household premises is provided to only 20% of the urban population, requiring significant improvement in service levels. Only 57% of the urban population have access to improved sanitation facilities in 2010 (56% for the whole country), which is lower than the average in South Asia. Bangladesh is not on track to meet the sanitation target on Millennium Development Goals. The situation is even more serious in slums, as the access to sanitation is highly correlated with wealth. Solid waste management is not systematic, and wastes are often dumped in open areas creating public health risks. Drainage is underdeveloped and poorly maintained. Although improvements are being made through earlier projects, including the UGIIP, most pourashavas still need significant investment support to improve their service delivery.

Impact: More people enjoying improved municipal services in target pourashavas

Outcome: Improved access to municipal services and strengthened pro-poor and gender-responsive urban governance in target pourashavas

Outputs:
1. Municipal infrastructure improved and made climate responsive in target pourashavas.
2. Community participation, accountability, and financial management systems strengthened with emphasis on gender equality and social inclusion.
3. Project management and administration adequately supported.
Business Opportunities:

- Consulting Services: A firm and individual consultants will be recruited in accordance with ADB's Guidelines on the Use of Consultants (2010, as amended from time to time). Consulting firms will be recruited using Quality and Cost-Based Selection (QCBS) method with a quality:cost ratio of 80:20. Advance contracting and retroactive financing will be considered.

- Procurement: All procurement to be financed under the project will be carried out in accordance with ADB's Procurement Guidelines (2010, as amended from time to time). Advance contracting and retroactive financing will be considered.

Responsible ADB Officer: Norio Saito (E-mail: nsaito@adb.org)
South Asia Department
Urban Development and Water Division, SARD

I. Second Public-Private Infrastructure Development Facility (PPIDF II)

Project No.	:	42180-013 (Proposed)
Amount (US $ million)	:	110
Executing Agencies	:	**Ministry of Finance**
Sector	:	**Mutisector**

Status: Management Review Meeting on 16 July 2013

Project Rationale and Linkage to Country/Regional Strategy: The proposed Second Public-Private Infrastructure Development Facility (PPIDF II or the "Project") will build on the efforts of PPIDF I in helping address the infrastructure deficiencies in Bangladesh by providing long-term debt financing and catalyzing private sector participation through Infrastructure Development Company Limited (IDCOL), and thereby supporting poverty reduction through enhanced investment, economic growth, and increase in employment opportunities. The design of the Project serves to attract commercial financing, thereby reducing the pressure on the public budget. An additional objective of the Project is to help provide the rural population and small to medium enterprises in off-grid areas with access to environment-friendly electricity. While PPIDF II represents a continuation of the first facility, it builds on lessons learnt from PPIDF I and includes new features such as: (i) the proposed incentive structure to move solar home system (SHS) technology towards using more energy-efficient light-emitting diode (LED) lights and (ii) the reduction of total project cost size from $30 million to $20 million for eligible sub-projects to facilitate the financing of a larger number of medium to large size infrastructure projects. More specifically, component 1 will enhance IDCOL's foreign currency resources to provide commercial financing to medium to large-sized private sector-led infrastructure projects with a total project cost of at least $20 million. Component 2 will provide Asian Development Fund (ADF) financing to IDCOL for the further expansion of its successful SHS program which has so far provided financing of more than 1 million SHS through a microfinance-based, direct sales program. Component 3 will provide ADF funding for IDCOL's ongoing RE program by financing RE applications-other than solar-such as biogas, biomass, and wind energy installations.

<u>Business Opportunities</u>:
- Consulting Services: To be determined

- Procurement Notices: To be determined

Responsible ADB Officer: Peter Marro (E-mail: pmarro@adb.org)
South Asia Department
Public Management, Financial Sector and Trade Division, SARD

J. Coastal Towns Infrastructure Improvement Project

Project No.   :   **44212-013 (Proposed)**
Amount (US $ million) :   **52**
Executing Agencies   :   **Local Government Engineering Department**
Sector   :   **Water Supply and Sanitation**

Status: Management Review Meeting on 16 September 2013

Description: The project takes a holistic and integrated approach to urban environmental improvement in vulnerable Bangladesh's coastal towns, which suffer deficits in basic urban services and are severely at risk to the impacts of climate change. It will provide climate resilient municipal infrastructure, including water supply, sanitation, drainage, flood protection, urban roads, and solid waste management facilities, and will strengthen institutional capacity and local governance for operating, maintaining, and expanding access to such services. The project will also mainstream climate resilience into urban planning. The Local Government Engineering Department (LGED), with extensive experience in managing Asian Development Bank (ADB) and other donor supported urban projects, will be the Executing Agency for the Project. Climate change and variability are critical development issues for Bangladesh, particularly in its low lying coastal areas naturally exposed to sea level rise, storm surges, and more frequent and intense storm events. The government, in its Sixth Five-Year Plan, FY2011 FY2015, has targeted assistance to vulnerable coastal populations with improvements in climate resilient water supply, sanitation, drainage, and flood protection infrastructure. The project was prioritized in the government s 2010 Strategic Program for Climate Resilience (SPCR), prepared under the Pilot Program for Climate Resilience (PPCR). As a key component of the SPCR, the project is eligible for financing from the Strategic Climate Fund (SCF) within the multi-donor coordinated Climate Investment Funds (CIF) as a pilot project for demonstrating ways to mainstream climate resilience into development. The coastal areas of Bangladesh consist of three distinct regions, namely the western, central and eastern zones comprising 19 districts. The coastal towns, with population of around 7 million, include both smaller pourashavas (secondary towns) and larger cities such as Khulna, Chittagong, and Barisal. Infrastructure is currently inadequate in these areas as they are either damaged by natural disasters or otherwise no longer functioning effectively. Weak local governance and municipal management coupled with high poverty incidence, and remote locations, create persistent development challenges to these areas. Climate change, variability, and natural disasters further aggravate development in coastal towns, with disproportionate impacts to women and the poor. The increased incidence of drought and saline intrusion (from sea level rise and storm surges) into groundwater, coupled with high non-revenue water, is posing serious risks to drinking water supplies, requiring the potential for developing new, but costlier, water supply sources located at far distances. Poor access to sanitation in coastal towns is also posing serious public and environmental health risks (Bangladesh is currently behind in achieving its MDG Target 10 indicators for urban sanitation). Drainage systems are underdeveloped and poorly maintained, and would be made further obsolete under more intense and frequent storm events. Given this scenario, future investments in urban infrastructure need to be climate-resilient to manage the long-term costs of investments, and to ensure that such investments deliver their intended benefits.

Project Rationale and Linkage to Country/Regional Strategy: The project will take a participatory approach to address the social, environmental, and institutional constraints to inclusive development in coastal towns, and will serve to pilot new approaches in climate adaption to be scaled up under future investments. It will reflect lessons learned from the first and second Urban Governance and Infrastructure Improvement (Sector) Projects (UGIIP), TA 7197 Strengthening Resilience of the Water Sector in Khulna to Climate Change, TA 7848 Climate Change Capacity Building and Knowledge Management, and recommendations from the ongoing CDTA 7890 Strengthening the Resilience of the Urban Water Supply, Drainage, and Sanitation to Climate Change in Coastal Towns related to the location of water-intake works, the appropriate design of drainage systems, and urban wastewater discharge. The project will also closely coordinate with the World Bank and other donors working in the urban sector to avoid duplication and ensure complementarities. ADB's Country Operations Business Plan (2012 2014) lists the Coastal Towns Infrastructure Improvement Project for implementation in 2013. The project is consistent with ADB's Bangladesh Country Partnership Strategy (2011-2015) which targets assistance to vulnerable coastal areas in adapting to the risks of climate change, as well as ADB s urban and water operational plans.

Impact: Improved health in coastal town populations

Outcome: Improved access to more reliable and climate-resilient municipal services in coastal towns

Outputs:
1. Improved municipal infrastructure with climate-resilient design in coastal towns
2. Strengthened local governance and capacity for sustainable service delivery and urban planning
3. Awareness raising and behavioral change programs implemented
4. Project management and administration support established

Business Opportunities:
- Consulting Services: A firm and individual consultants will be recruited in accordance with ADB s Guidelines on the Use of Consultants (2010, as amended from time to time). Consulting firms will be recruited using Quality and Cost-Based Selection (QCBS) method with a quality:cost ratio of 80:20.

- Procurement: All procurement to be financed under the project will be carried out in accordance with ADB s Procurement Guidelines (2010, as amended from time to time).

Responsible ADB Officer: Ron H. Slangen (E-mail: rslangen@adb.org)
South Asia Department
Urban Development and Water Division, SARD

BHUTAN

A. Green Power Development Project II

Project No.	:	**44444-013 (Proposed)**
Amount (US $ million)	:	**182**
Executing Agencies	:	**Department of Energy**
Sector	:	**Multisector**

Status: Management Review Meeting on 1 July 2014

Description: The project outputs include: (i) operation of a 210 MW run-of-the-river Nikachhu hydropower plant and its associated transmission lines, and (ii) enhanced institutional capacity of DGPC in financial, social, and environmental terms. The project will generate power of 903,490 MWh on the average annually. Power generated is expected to be exported by Indian power trader(s) to neighboring countries including India and Bangladesh through the existing grid connected to India and planned one to Bangladesh. Given that clean and renewable power export will be counted as carbon saving, the resulting reduction of greenhouse gases equivalent to CO_2 emissions is estimated around 1,000,000 tons every year assuming on the Indian grid system benchmark.

Project Rationale and Linkage to Country/Regional Strategy: In 2008, ADB approved financing the Green Power Development Project for Bhutan to mainly promote the Dagachhu hydropower development (114

MW) for power export to India, through a public private partnership (PPP). While the cross-border power trading has physically been limited only between Bhutan and India in South Asia, ADB also decided to finance the transmission interconnection between Bangladesh and India in August 2010. These projects have created potential to expand power trading from the cross-border to regional dimension. The Green Power Development Project-II (the Project) is proposed to export Bhutan's hydropower to both Bangladesh and India through Indian power trader(s). The Project is a medium size run-of-the-river type (210 MW) which will have small environmental and social impacts unlike reservoir types. It is located on the Nikachhu River in Trongsa of the central Bhutan. The Government of Bhutan officially requested ADB for the project on 6 September 2010. Bhutan is the only South Asian country with a surplus of power for export. While there is seasonal demand and supply gaps particularly in dry winters, the country's annual generation capacity (around 1,500 MW) is significantly greater than its domestic demand; Bhutan is a net power exporter. Of total power generated, around 80% is exported to India as of 2010. Power exports account for more than 40% of national revenue and 25% of gross domestic product (GDP) in Bhutan. Hydropower infrastructure development also contributes another 25% of GDP through the construction sector. The revenue from power exports are the primary source for the government's socioeconomic development for health, education, agriculture and rural development. The hydropower development thus forms the backbone of Bhutan's economy and social lives. Bhutan's potential hydropower is 23,760 MW, 6% of which has been exploited to meet domestic consumption and the remainder is for export. On the other hand, neighboring countries including India and Bangladesh are experiencing a large power supply deficit and their power sources are dominated by fossil fuel-based thermal generation plants with greenhouse gas emission. Clean energy development for power export from Bhutan will increase energy supply stability, improve energy efficiency, and foster climate change mitigation on the sub-regional level. The development of a transmission interconnection between Bangladesh and India is expected to expand the subregional network potential. Given the fact that Bhutan has recently faced with shortage of power during the winter periods due to fast growing domestic demand and reduction of river water flows in the dry seasons, Bhutan also has economic incentives to import power from the neighboring countries during the lean seasons through the cross-border network. To establish the complementary relationship of power supply among the three countries and to diversify potential buyers and sellers are expected to step forward to a regional power trading market in a competitive environment and strengthen energy security with each other. Trilateral energy trade in the sub-region will eventually contribute to economic growth through deeper regional integration.

Impact: Increased power trading among Bhutan, Bangladesh and India

Outcome: Sub-regional commercial power trading platform created

Outputs: Nikachhu hydropower generation plant is operational DGPC' s institutional capacity is enhanced financially, socially, and environmentally.

Business Opportunities:
- Consulting Services: To be determined

- Procurement Notices: To be determined

Responsible ADB Officer: Kaoru Ogino (E-mail: kogino@adb.org)
South Asia Department
Energy Division, SARD

B. SASEC Road Connectivity Project (formerly Road Network Project II [Additional Financing])

Project No.   :   39225-034 (Proposed)
Amount (US $ million) :   40
Executing Agencies   :   Department of Roads
Sector   :   Transport and ICT

Status: Management Review Meeting on 15 July 2013

Description: The proposed Project will be a scale up of RNP II, and its objectives include enhancing the country's road transport connectivity by improving access to regional and global markets throughout the country. The Project will concentrate on expanding the country's road network by continuing construction of segments of the second east-west highway. It will enhance the project impact, outcome and outputs of RNP II to assist Bhutan's long term infrastructure plan of realizing the second east-west highway in the south.

Impact: Industrial development and regional trade promoted in the southern economic hubs

Outcome: Efficient, safe, and expanded capacity of road transport infrastructure in the southern region of Bhutan with India and through India to Bangladesh and Nepal

Outputs: Critical sections connected along the southern east-west corridor

Business Opportunities:
  ▪   Consulting Services: To be determined

  ▪   Procurement Notices: To be determined

Responsible ADB Officer: Tsuneyuki Sakai (E-mail: tsakai@adb.org)
                                    South Asia Department
                                    Transport and Communications Division, SARD

CAMBODIA

A. Third Financial Sector Program - Subprogram 2

Loan No.   :   3002
Project No.   :   42305-023
Amount (US $ million) :   15
Executing Agencies   :   National Bank of Cambodia
Sector   :   Finance

Status: Board approved on 14 May 2013

Description: The sequence of financial reforms in Cambodia has been guided by the Government's 10-year FSDS. A project preparatory technical assistance (PPTA) for $850,000 ($700,000 from ADB TASF IV) was approved in April 2010 to help the Government update the FSDS 2006-2015 and formulate the next cluster program. IMF and World Bank have recently completed the first financial sector assessment program (FSAP) on Cambodia that will provide useful inputs to the update of the 10-year FSDS. While FSP I has been rated successful by the independent evaluation department (IED), some of the reform measures were not widely enforced due to weak inter-ministerial coordination and capacity constraint. Prepared within the framework of the updated FSDS, the next program cluster (FSP III) will help complete some of the reform programs that commenced during FSP II, strengthen the enforcement of completed activities, and commence reform activities in leasing, capital market, and pension fund. The expected overall impact of the cluster program is a sound, market-based finance sector to enhance mobilization of financial resources to support sustainable economic growth. The expected outcome of the FSP III is a growing, resilient, and efficient financial system. FSP III is expected to be approved in November 2011. The National Bank of Cambodia will be the Executing Agency, and the Ministry of Economy and Finance (MEF) and Ministry of Commerce (MOC) will be the Implementing Agencies.

Project Rationale and Linkage to Country/Regional Strategy: The Government of Cambodia requested a program loan from the Asian Development Bank (ADB) during program consultations in 2009 to support Cambodia's on-going reforms of its finance sector. ADB has supported reforms in Cambodia's finance sector since 1999. As the finance sector moves towards a sound market oriented system, the proposed program will ensure that the momentum will not be lost on reforms initiated under the two ADB Financial Sector Programs (FSP I and II). The development of Cambodia's finance sector is one of five core areas that best support ADB's Strategy 2020 and its goal to reduce poverty in Cambodia. This is in line with the priority outlined in the Government's 5-year National Strategic Development Plan (NSDP) 2006-2010 and the draft NSDP 2011-2013. The proposed program cluster for a total of $45 million (ADF) was included in the country operations business plan (COBP) 2009-2012. The development framework for Cambodia's finance sector is based on the 10-year Financial Sector Development Strategy 2001-2010 that was updated as the FSDS 2006-2015 and adopted by the Government in February 2007. Through ADB's first Financial Sector Program (FSP I) that commenced in 2001 and concluded in August 2007, the Government was able to lay the legal and regulatory foundations necessary for a sound, market-oriented financial sector. The government also took strong measures to consolidate the banking system and introduce more stringent requirements for capital adequacy, governance, and risk management. With positive results after FSP I, and to ensure the durability of its reform program and greater accessibility to financial services by ordinary citizens, the Government requested continuing ADB support to the sector. This led to the design and approval of the FSP II in 2007. FSP II with a series of four single-tranche subprograms, commenced in September 2006 and completed in December 2010. FSP II helped to strengthen resilience, improve public confidence, improve financial intermediation, strengthen competition in the financial markets, ease financing constraints, update the associated legal and regulatory framework, and establish key financial infrastructures.

Impact: A sound, market-oriented finance sector to enhance the mobilization of financial resources

Outcome: A growing, resilient, and efficient financial system

Outputs: Finance sector efficiency enhanced Finance Sector stability maintained Confidence and financial intermediation improved Good governance promoted

Business Opportunities:
- Consulting Services: To be determined

- Procurement Notices: To be determined

Responsible ADB Officer: Hiroyuki Aoki (E-mail: haoki@adb.org)
                          Southeast Asia Department
                          Public Management, Financial Sector and Trade Division, SERD

B. Public-Private Partnership Development Project
Project No. : 46493-001 (Proposed)
Amount (US $ million) : 0.9
Sector : **Transport and ICT**

Status: Management Review Meeting on 15 July 2013

Impact: Increase private sector investment in infrastructure to accelerate Cambodia s economic growth

Outcome: Improved enabling environment to catalyze PPPs and infrastructure investments

Business Opportunities:
Consulting Services: To be determined

Procurement Notices: To be determined

Responsible ADB Officer: Bob Finlayson (E-mail: bfinlayson@adb.org)
Southeast Asia Department
Public Management, Financial Sector and Trade Division, SERD

C. Urban Water Supply and Sanitation (formerly Rural Water Supply and Sanitation Project III)
Project No. : 41403-013 (Proposed)
Amount (US $ million) : 15
Sector : **Water Supply and Sanitation**

Status: Management Review Meeting scheduled on 15 August 2013

Impact: Expanded access to sustainable and safe water supply services for the urban population in Cambodia

Outcome: Improved water supply infrastructure and service provision in selected provincial waterworks.

Outputs:
1. Water treatment plants provided or improved
2. Water distribution systems improved and coverage increased
3. Existing pumping stations rehabilitated
4. Institutional capacity of MIME and regulatory system strengthened

Business Opportunities:
- Consulting Services: To be determined

- Procurement Notices: To be determined

Responsible ADB Officer: Michael E. White (E-mail: mewhite@adb.org)
Southeast Asia Department
Urban Development and Water Division, SERD

D. Climate Resilient Rice Commercialization Sector Development Program

Loan No.	:	3006, 3007
Grant No.	:	0349, 0350
Project No.	:	44321-013
Amount (US $ million)	:	55
Executing Agencies	:	Ministry of Economy and Finance
		Ministry of Agriculture, Forestry & Fisheries
Sector	:	Multisector

Status: Board approval scheduled on June 27, 2013

Description: The Climate Resilient Rice Commercialization Sector Development Program (SDP) is proposed to support and accelerate the efficient and effective implementation of the Strategy on Agriculture and Water (SAW) and the Policy on the Promotion of Paddy Production and Rice Export (the Rice Policy). It will address food security and rice commercialization by prioritizing: (i) strengthening the rice value chain; (ii) improving the legal and regulatory framework in agricultural land management; (iii) improving access to credit by paddy producers and rice millers/exporters; and (iv) enhancing paddy production and productivity through improved irrigation water use efficiency, establishment of paddy post-harvesting facilities, and paddy crop insurance pilots. The SDP will: (i) address major strategic thrusts of the 2011 - 2013 Country Partnership Strategy, and sector strategies and roadmap; and (ii) complement the on-going sector initiatives by emphasizing the commercialization aspects of rice.

Impact: Increased Net Incomes of Stakeholders along the Rice Value Chain

Outcome: Enhanced Production of Quality Rice in Cambodia while preserving the natural resource base

Outputs:
- A Conducive Legal and Regulatory Environment Established to Facilitate Rice Commercialization
- Agricultural Land-use Zoning Improved
- Climate Resilient Rice Value Chain Infrastructure Developed
- Enhanced Rice Value Chain Support Services to Improve Quality of Cambodian Rice
- Weather-indexed Crop Insurance (WICI) Piloted
- Efficient Program Management and Implementation

Business Opportunities:
- Consulting Services: The project preparatory technical assistance (PPTA) will require 42 person months of international consultants and 53 person months of national consultant. ADB will engage, on an individual basis, four international consultants for a total of 13 person-months and four national consultants for a total of 12 person-months. The remaining international consultants (29 person months) and national consultants (41 person months) will be engaged through a firm, or association of firms. The ADB will engage all the consultants in accordance with ADB's Guidelines on the Use of Consultants (2010, as amended from time to time).

- Procurement: Procurement packages will be determined on the basis of the project design.

Responsible ADB Officer: Bui Minh Giap (E-mail: buigm@adb.org)
Southeast Asia Department
Environment, Natural Resources & Agriculture Division, SERD

CHINA

A. Jiangxi Ji'an Sustainable Urban Transport Project

Project No.	:	45022-002 (Proposed)
Amount (US $ million) :		120
Sector	:	Transport and ICT

Status: Management Review Meeting on 21 April 2013

Impact: A safe, efficient and more environmentally sustainable urban transport system is established.

Outcome: Efficient multimodal accessibility to the new main railway station is established.

Outputs:
1. Public transport hub constructed
2. Station access roads completed
3. Bus Rapid Transit system established
4. Station square constructed
5. Green zone completed
6. Energy efficiency measures completed

Business Opportunities:
-   Consulting Services: To be determined

-   Procurement Notices: To be determined

Responsible ADB Officer: Steven Lewis-Workman (E-mail: slworkman@adb.org)
East Asia Department
Transport and Communications Division, EARD

B. Yuxi-Mohan Subregional Railway Link Project

Project No.	:	45031-002 (Proposed)
Amount (US $ million) :		150
Sector	:	Transport and ICT

Status: Management Review Meeting on 19 Jun 2013

Impact: A sustainable and efficient railway transport system developed in Yunnan province

Outcome: Improved efficient and low-carbon railway system in Yunnan that further connect to greater Mekong Subregion (GMS) countries

Outputs:
1. Completed subregional railway infrastructure and associated facilities
2. Energy efficiency, emissions reduction, and safety enhancement
3. Jinghong multimodal passenger hub
4. Tourism facilities completed

5. Yuxi-Mohan subregional logistics corridor formed

Business Opportunities:
- Consulting Services: To be determined

- Procurement Notices: To be determined

Responsible ADB Officer: Xiaoxin Chen (E-mail: xchen@adb.org)
East Asia Department
Transport and Communications Division, EARD

C. Jilin Urban Services Improvement Project

Project No.	:	**46048-002 (Proposed)**
Amount (US $ million)	:	**150**
Executing Agencies	:	**Jilin Provincial Government**
Sector	:	**Multisector**

Status: Management Review Meeting on 19 August 2014

Description: The proposed project will support the development of Baishan and Baicheng Cities in Jilin Province, the People s Republic of China (PRC) as livable and resource efficient medium-sized cities. It will address urgent infrastructure needs and make provision for: (i) streamlining integrated solid waste management (ISWM) based on 3R principles; (ii) improving water supply services in Baishan; and (iii) constructing urban road with associated facilities in Baicheng.
Impact: Improved quality of life in Baishan and Baicheng Cities

Outcome: Improved delivery of municipal services in Baishan and Baicheng Cities

Outputs:
- Efficient ISWM system in Baishan and Baicheng Cities
- Improved water supply management in Baishan City
- Improved coverage of urban roads and municipal services in Baicheng City
- Improved capacity and institutional arrangement

Business Opportunities:
- Consulting Services: In accordance with ADB's Guidelines on the Use of Consultants (2010, as amended from time to time), a consulting firm will be engaged using the quality- and cost-based selection method with a ratio of 90:10 using the simplified technical proposal procedure.

- Procurement Notices: To be determined

Responsible ADB Officer: Arnaud Heckmann (E-mail: aheckmann@adb.org)
East Asia Department
Urban and Social Sectors Division, EARD

D. Hubei-Yichang Sustainable Urban Transport Project

Project No.	:	45023-002 (Proposed)
Amount (US $ million)	:	150
Executing Agencies	:	Yichang Municipality Government
Sector	:	Transport and ICT

Status: Management Review Meeting on 16 April 2013

Description: The Hubei-Yichang Municipal Government proposes a project with the following components: (i) road reconstruction and installation of bus rapid transit (BRT) corridor (18 kilometers [km]), (ii) establishing BRT services; (iii) construction of two road sections (24.7 km) to support logistics park development and to accommodate increasing pass-dam transshipment demand; and (iv) support for non-motorized transport (NMT), travel demand management (TDM) in Yichang central business district (CBD) through parking management. The proposed Project is aligned with the key thrusts of ADB's assistance to the PRC under the PRC Country Partnership Strategy (CPS) in the areas of: (i) inclusive growth and balanced development by promoting urbanization in less developed regions, and (ii) resource efficiency and environmental sustainability by promoting efficient and sustainable urban transport and transit-oriented development. The focus on public transport and multi-modal integration fits well with ADB's Sustainable Transport Initiative (STI)

Project Rationale and Linkage to Country/Regional Strategy: Yichang is facing two main transport challenges. The first challenge is to develop its transport system to support urban and industrial development in a sustainable way. The main districts, industrial sites, stations, and terminals need to be served by efficient public transport services to reduce transport cost, provide increased accessibility to jobs and services, and promote economic development. Currently bus services have no lane priority and the route structure is not adequately serving the city. The second challenge is to enhance the logistics hub function of Yichang by providing efficient accessibility to the logistic parks being developed in the city, and provide means of meeting the increasing demand for pass-dam transshipment. An efficient logistics hub function and increased pass-dam transshipment capacity will decrease logistics costs and environmental costs around the region by enabling increased use of inland waterways.

Impact: Sustainable and convenient urban transport and efficient logistics systems are built in Yichang City

Outcome: Sustainable and efficient transport system for public transport and logistics is provided.

Outputs:
1. BRT corridor built
2. TDM measures implemented
3. NMT measures implemented
4. Road network improvements constructed

Business Opportunities:
- Consulting Services: To be determined

- Procurement Notices: To be determined

Responsible ADB Officer: Ki-Joon Kim (E-mail: kjkim@adb.org)
East Asia Department
Transport and Communications Division, EARD

E. Yunnan Sustainable Road Maintenance Project

Project No.   :   45030-002 (Proposed)
Amount (US $ million) :   80
Sector   :   Transport and ICT

Status: Management Review Meeting on 18 October 2012

Impact: An accessible, affordable and safe transport system developed in Yunnan Province

Outcome: Improved road asset management in Yunnan Province

Outputs:
1. Road maintenance and rehabilitation program implemented
2. Good road maintenance implementation practices piloted
3. Institutional capacity to manage YHAB roads is strengthened

Business Opportunities:
- Consulting Services: To be determined

- Procurement Notices: To be determined

Responsible ADB Officer: Adrien Veron-Okamoto (E-mail: averon@adb.org)
                           East Asia Department
                           Transport and Communications Division, EARD

F. Yunnan Chuxiong Urban Environment Improvement Project

Project No.   :   45507-003 (Proposed)
Amount (US $ million) :   150
Sector   :   Transport and ICT

Status: Management Review Meeting scheduled on 23 September 2013

Project details yet to be released by ADB.

Business Opportunities:
- Consulting Services: To be determined

- Procurement: To be determined

Responsible ADB Officer: Satoshi Ishii (E-mail: sishii@adb.org)
                           East Asia Department
                           Urban and Social Sectors Division, EARD

G. Anhui Huainan Urban Water Systems Integrated Rehabilitation Project

Project No.   :   46078-002 (Proposed)
Amount (US $ million) :   150
Executing Agencies   :   Huainan Municipal Govenment
Sector   :   Multisector

Status: Management Review Meeting scheduled on 4 July 2013

Description: The impact of the project will be improved urban water environment, public health, and quality of life for urban residents in the Huainan municipality. The outcome of the project will be improved management of surface water resources in the Huainan municipality. The project will have the following components which are all linked to each other:

- Component 1: Improvement of wastewater collection and transmission systems. This component will include installation of 115.2-kilometer (km) new main wastewater collection and transmission pipes in the eastern area of the Huainan municipality, and installation of 63.7-km new main wastewater collection and transmission pipes and construction of three new pump stations for wastewater transmission in the western area.
- Component 2: Improvement of urban water channels. This component will include improvement of existing 7.6-km Bagongshang water channel, 8.7-km Xiejiaji water channel, 13.8-km Donghua water channel, 0.5-km Old Longwang water channel, and 3.5-km Longwang water channel; and construction of a new 8.1-km Longwang flood diversion water channel. Activities under this component will include: (i) sludge removal from the five existing urban water channels; (ii) improvement or construction of the water channels to improve the urban water environment and increase flood flow capacity to meet 1/20 year-level storm water; (iii) installation of new wastewater collection and transmission pipes along the channels to intercept wastewater inflow into the channels; and (iv) promotion of international best practices of nonstructural measures, such as reduction of garbage dumping along the channels and their tributaries; setting and securing of environmental flow in the channels; sustainable maintenance of the channels; monitoring of water quality and ecosystem; and capacity and institutional strengthening.
- Component 3: Improvement of lakes and wetlands. This component will include two subcomponents. Subcomponent 3.1: Increase of flood control capacities will include construction of 13-km embankments and four pump stations along Gaotang Lake, improvement of the Dajiangou and Long Lake pump stations, and reconstruction of the Caozhuizi and Shijian Lake pump stations to increase flood control capacities to meet 1/20 year-level storm water. Subcomponent 3.2: Improvement of water environment will include improvement of water environment in Gaotang Lake, Dajiangou wetland, Long Lake, Caoling Lake, and Shijian Lake. Activities to improve water environment may include, but are not limited to, (i) sludge removal (footnote 3); (ii) plantation for water self-purification; and (iii) promotion of international best practices of nonstructural measures, such as monitoring of water quality and ecosystem; species recovery; public awareness raising and education; and capacity and institutional strengthening. Component 4: Project management support and capacity development. Activities under this component will include (i) consultants support for project management; (ii) institutional and capacity strengthening for project management, and operation and maintenance of the infrastructure; and (iii) provision of equipment for project management.

Impact: Improved urban water environment, public health, and quality of life for urban residents in Huainan municipality

Outcome: Improved management of surface water resources in Huainan municipality

Outputs:
1. Wastewater collection systems improved
2. Urban water channels improved
3. Lakes and wetlands improved: (i) flood control capacities increased, and (ii) water environment improved
4. Project management support provided and capacity development undertaken

Business Opportunities:
- Consulting Services: Consultants will be required for the promotion of international best practices of nonstructural measures to improve water environment, and project management support and capacity development. All consultants will be hired following ADB's Guidelines on the Use of Consultants (2010, as amended from time to time).

- Procurement: All ADB-financed procurement will be conducted following ADB's Procurement Guidelines (2010, as amended from time to time). A procurement agency will be hired to conduct procurement on behalf of the implementing agencies.

Responsible ADB Officer: Yoshiaki Kobayashi (E-mail: yoshikobayashi@adb.org)
East Asia Department
Environment, Natural Resources & Agriculture Division, EARD

H. Jiangxi Zhelin Lake Water Resources Integrated Utilization Project

Project No.	:	**46080-002 (Proposed)**
Amount (US $ million)	:	**100**
Executing Agencies	:	**Jiujiang Municipal Development and Reform Com.**
Sector	:	**Multisector**

Status: Management Review Meeting scheduled on 26 September 2013

Impact: Improved sustainability of socio-economic growth in Jiujiang Municipality

Outcome: Reliable and sustainable secondary water source for Jiujiang Municipality

Outputs: Improved watershed services at Zhelin Lake and Xiu River Integrated utilization of water resources downstream of Zhelin Lake Enhanced water supply infrastructure in Jiujiang Municipality Strengthened institutional and management capacity

Business Opportunities:
- Consulting Services: To be determined

- Procurement Notices: To be determined

Responsible ADB Officer: Qingfeng Zhang (E-mail: qingfengzhang@adb.org)
East Asia Department
Environment, Natural Resources & Agriculture Division, EARD

I. Hubei Huanggang Integrated Urban Environment Improvement Project

Project No.	:	46050-002 (Proposed)
Amount (US $ million)	:	100
Executing Agencies	:	Huanggang Municipal Government
Sector	:	Multisector

Status: Management Review Meeting on 31 January 2014

Description: The proposed project aims to promote environmentally sustainable and socially inclusive urbanization in Huanggang Municipality in Hubei Province, the People's Republic of China (PRC) through improvements in urban environmental infrastructure and management services. The project will support urban lake and river enhancement, solid waste management, urban roads and associated utility networks, and capacity development of related urban services. Huanggang is located in eastern Hubei Province, approximately 78 kilometers (km) away from the provincial capital of Wuhan. Huanggang is the second most populated municipality in Hubei Province with 7.46 million residents. Building on traditionally rural-based economy, Huanggang is the poorest municipality in the province and has relatively low urbanization rate of 35.7%. Huanggang Municipal Government (HMG), in its Twelfth Five-Year Plan (12th FYP), targets to transform its economic structure and facilitate urbanization with expanded secondary and tertiary industries.

Project Rationale and Linkage to Country/Regional Strategy: The project aligns with ADB's 2011-2015 country partnership strategy for the PRC, promoting sustainable and environment-friendly urban development. It will support economically and socially inclusive urbanization and rural-urban transition in Huanggang and contribute to balanced regional development in the PRC as well as in Hubei Province, thereby supporting the PRC's 12th FYP. The project will build on ADB's experiences and lessons gained from previous urban projects in Hubei, and various policy-oriented technical assistance projects and knowledge products on water resources management, wetlands, climate change adaptation, and small- and medium-sized cities' development in the PRC.

Impact: Socially inclusive and environmentally sustainable urbanization in Huanggang

Outcome: Improved urban environmental infrastructure and management services in Huanggang

Outputs:
- Lakes and rivers are enhanced with environment facilities operating
- Solid waste collection and transfer facilities are operating
- Urban roads are opened to traffic and related services are operating
- Capacity developed and institutions strengthened

Business Opportunities:
- Consulting Services: The PMO and HUCIC will be assisted by project implementation consultants for project management and institutional capacity building. Consulting services will be engaged in accordance with ADB's Guidelines on the Use of Consultants (2010, as amended from time to time).

- Procurement: To be determined;;all procurement of goods and works will be undertaken in accordance with ADB's Procurement Guidelines (2010, as amended from time to time).

Responsible ADB Officer: Gyongshim An (E-mail: gyongshiman@adb.org)
East Asia Department
Urban and Social Sectors Division, EARD

J. Guangdong Chaonan Water Resources Development and Protection Demonstration Project

Project No.	:	46079-002 (Proposed)
Amount (US $ million)	:	100
Executing Agencies	:	Guangdong Provincial Government (GPG)
Sector	:	Multisector

Status: Management Review Meeting scheduled on 27 September 2013

Description: The expected impact of the project will be sustained economic development in Chaonan District. The outcome of the project will be improved and equitable water supply services inclusive of urban and rural residents in Chaonan District. The project will include four outputs: (i) improved water resources protection, (ii) inclusive urban and rural water supply system, (iii) increased awareness on environment and sanitation, and (iv) strengthened institutional and staff capacity.

- Improved water resources protection. This output will support: (i) reforestation around the three major reservoir areas in the district; (ii) research on pollution prevention and control measures in the reservoir areas; and (iii) pilot programs on solid waste collection and treatment, and nonpoint source pollution control.
- Inclusive urban and rural water supply system. This output will support: (i) the expansion of the capacity of two water supply plants (Quifeng and Jinxi) from 110,000 cubic meters per day to 182,000 cubic meters per day; (ii) the construction of the Longxi water supply plant with a capacity of 100,000 cubic meters per day; (iii) rehabilitation and newly installation of water delivery and distribution pipelines, including an integrated system connecting the three water supply systems; (iv) construction of an operational center for the integrated water supply system; and (v) establishment of about 40 small-scale water supply facilities for rural residents in hilly areas.
- Increased awareness on environment and sanitation. This output will support the development of education and training materials for schools, training of school teachers, public awareness campaign, training equipment, and media communication.
- Strengthened institutional and staff capacity. This output will: (i) provide training, workshops, and study tours; (ii) establish a water quality monitoring center; (iii) develop a monitoring and regulatory system for dam safety and reservoir operations; and (iv) formulate two plans on water resources development and management, and pollution control; and (v) establish a proper operational model for the water supply company aligned to the new integrated water supply system.

Business Opportunities:
- Consulting Services: It is estimated that about 18 person-months of staff time will be required to prepare the project. A project preparatory technical assistance (PPTA) is requested to help prepare the proposed project that would be compliant with ADB's and the government s requirements. It is expected that 12 person-months of international and 32 person-months of national consultants are required. The consultants will support the executing and implementing agencies in completing the project feasibility studies and safeguard documents to a standard consistent with the requirements of ADB and the government. The consultants will also provide start-up project implementation support to the executing and implementing agencies. ADB's Guidelines on the Use of Consultants (2010, as amended from time to time) will be applied in recruiting consultants.

- Procurement Notices: To be determined

Responsible ADB Officer: Zhou Yaozhou (E-mail: yaozhou@adb.org)
East Asia Department
Environment, Natural Resources & Agriculture Division, EARD

K. Yunnan Pu'er Regional Integrated Road Network Development Project

Project No.   :   46040-003 (Proposed)
Amount (US $ million) :   200
Sector   :   Transport and ICT

Status: Management Review Meeting scheduled on 5 November 2013

Impact: Regional integration and trade between Yunnan Pu'er and neighboring countries is enhanced

Outcome: Accessibility between rural and border areas and the regional transport network in Yunnan Pu'er is improved

Outputs:
1. Rural roads upgraded from earthen roads to paved Class IV standards
2. Ning er-Jiangcheng-Longfu road rehabilitated to Class IV and Class III standards
3. Simao-Ning er road constructed to Class II standards
4. Community development

Business Opportunities:
  ▪   Consulting Services: To be determined

  ▪   Procurement Notices: To be determined

Responsible ADB Officer: Steven Lewis-Workman (E-mail: slworkman@adb.org)
                            East Asia Department
                            Transport and Communications Division, EARD

L. Anhui Intermodal Sustainable Transport Development Project

Project No.   :   45021-002 (Proposed)
Amount (US $ million) :   200
Executing Agencies   :   Anhui Provincial Government
Sector   :   Transport and ICT

Status: Management Review Meeting scheduled on 17 September 2013

Impact: An environmentally sustainable and multimodal transport system developed in Anhui province

Outcome: An efficient, safe and affordable multimodal transport system developed in Wangjiang Demonstration Zone

Outputs: Road network and safety improved Inland waterway network and safety improved Institutional capacity developed

Business Opportunities:
  ▪   Consulting Services: The project preparatory technical assistance (PPTA) will be implemented using a combination of individual consultants and an international consulting firm. Individual consultants will be engaged for selected activities such as road safety and logistics.

- Procurement: All procurement to be financed under the ADB loan will be carried out in accordance with ADB s Procurement Guidelines (2010, as amended from time to time). All consultant services will be recruited using quality and cost-based selection in accordance with ADB's Guidelines on the Use of Consultants (2010, as amended from time to time).

Responsible ADB Officer: Sharad Saxena (E-mail: ssaxena@adb.org)
East Asia Department
Transport and Communications Division, EARD

M. Inner Mongolia Road Development Project

Project No.   :   43029-013 (Proposed)
Amount (US $ million) :   200
Sector   :   Transport and ICT

Status: Management review meeting scheduled on 19 March 2013

Impact: Sustainable road transport system in Inner Mongolia to support the Regional Development Strategy

Outcome: A safe and efficient, road transport network in Hulunbeier is developed.

Outputs:
Highway upgrading and road safety improvements
Rehabilitation of rural roads
Cross border transport improvement and trade facilitation
Support for community based eco-tourism and environmental conservation

Status: Management Review Meeting on 19 March 2013

Business Opportunities:
- Consulting Services: To be determined

- Procurement: To be determined

Responsible ADB Officer: Sharad Saxena (E-mail: ssaxena@adb.org)
East Asia Department
Transport and Communications Division, EARD

N. Henan Value Chain and Products Safety Demonstration Project

Project No.   :   46081-002 (Proposed)
Amount (US $ million) :   80
Sector   :   Multisector

Status: Management Review Meeting on 29 October 2013

Impact: Improved safety of livestock products made in Henan province

Outcome: Sustainable livestock value chains demonstrated in project counties that deliver quality food

Outputs:

- Livestock product safety monitoring and testing system developed and operated
- Environmentally-sustainable livestock production and processing implemented
- Effective project management and monitoring

Business Opportunities:
- Consulting Services: To be determined

- Procurement: To be determined

Responsible ADB Officer: Takeshi Ueda (E-mail: taueda@adb.org)
East Asia Department
Environment, Natural Resources & Agriculture Division, EARD

O. Qinghai Delinha Concentrated Solar Energy Plant Project

Project No.	:	46058-002 (Proposed)
Amount (US $ million)	:	150
Executing Agencies	:	China Guangdong Nuclear Power Holding Co., Ltd.
Sector	:	Energy

Status: Management Review Meeting on 1 July 2013

Description: The proposed Qinghai Delinha Solar Thermal Plant Project (the Project) will construct 50 megawatt (MW) concentrating solar thermal power (CSP) plant in Qinghai Province. The Project is the first-of-its-kind utility scale CSP plant in the People's Republic of China (PRC). A project preparatory technical assistance (TA) will be undertaken for the due diligence of the Project.

Impact: Expanded share of CSP plants in renewable energy mix in the PRC

Outcome: Successful commercial operation of the utility scale CSP plant with thermal storage system in Qinghai province

Outputs: Construction of 50 MW CSP plant with thermal storage in Qinghai province

Business Opportunities:
- Consulting Services: The technical assistance (TA) will take a unique approach (two stages of consulting services) to use efficiently the limited loan processing time and to effectively guide the executing and implementing agency since the initial stage of project preparation, which is necessary to improve technical and financial viability of the proposed project. Part 1 (preliminary design review and technical guidance, initial financial viability assessment, and advance procurement support) will require a total of 5 person-months of three individual international consultants and 5 person-months of two individual national consultants while Part 2 (detailed due diligence, technical guidance, and capacity development) will require a total of 12 person-months of five international and 15 person-months of four national consulting services. Part 1 will be implemented while the selection of consulting services of Part 2 is underway. Early engagement of Part 1 consultant is essential to ensure quality of design, assess possible financial viability gap, and advance procurement support. The outputs delivered by the consultants of Part 1 will be carried over to the consultants of Part 2. All international and national consultants will be engaged by ADB in accordance with the Guidelines on the Use of Consultants (2010, as amended from time to time).

- Procurement: The procurement of equipment by consultants, under the TA, will follow ADBs Procurement Guidelines (2010, as amended from time to time). The proceeds of the TA will be disbursed in line with ADB's Technical Assistance Disbursement Handbook (2010, as amended from time to time).

Responsible ADB Officer: Shigeru Yamamura (E-mail: syamamura@adb.org)
East Asia Department
Energy Division, EARD

P. Xinjiang Integrated Urban Development

Project No.   :   **45508-002 (Proposed)**
Amount (US $ million) :   **200**
Executing Agencies :   **Government of Xinjiang Uygur Autonomous Region**
Sector   :   **Multisector**

Status: Management Review Meeting on 8 March 2013

Description: The project will improve urban infrastructure facilities and the environment in the cities of Kelamayi and Kuitun in the Xinjiang Uygur Autonomous Region (XUAR), which will contribute to sustainable economic growth and improve the quality of life for about 330,000 urban residents in the two project cities.

Impact: Improved living conditions and environmental sustainability in the cities of Kelamayi and Kuitun

Outcome: Improved urban management and services, including upgraded water, roads, and flood control in the project cities

Outputs:
1. Improvement of Kelayami's Urban Infrastructure
    1.1 Nanjiao wastewater treatment upgrading
    1.2 Wetland construction and treated wastewater storage
    1.3 Wastewater reuse
    1.4 New road construction
    1.5 Improved water management

2. Improvement of Kuitun's Urban Infrastructure
    2.1 City urban drainage channel flood management
    2.2 Improved water management

3. Project Management and Capacity Building Capacity to deliver municipal services to standards required under PRC regulations and in line with customer expectations

Business Opportunities:
  ▪ Consulting Services: All consultants will be recruited according to ADB's Guidelines on the Use of Consultants (2010, as amended from time to time). An estimated 124 person-months (9 international and 115 national) of consulting services are required to: (i) facilitate project management and implementation, and (ii) strengthen the institutional and operational capacity of the executing agency. Consulting firms will be engaged using the quality- and cost-based selection method with a standard quality: cost ratio of 80:20 and a full technical proposal will be required for the bidding.

  ▪ Procurement: All procurement of goods and works will be undertaken in accordance with ADB's Procurement Guidelines. International competitive bidding procedures will be used for civil works contracts estimated to exceed $10 million, and goods contracts estimated to exceed $1 million.

Contracts for goods and for works estimated to cost less than the above international competitive bidding threshold values, but more than $100,000 for goods and $100,000 for works, will be procured on the basis of national competitive bidding procedures in accordance with the People's Republic of China (PRC) Tendering and Bidding Law (1999), subject to modifications agreed upon with ADB. Shopping will be used for contracts for procurement of works and equipment worth less than $100,000 and $100,000, respectively.

Responsible ADB Officer: Sangay Penjor (E-mail: spenjor@adb.org)
East Asia Department
Urban and Social Sectors Division, EARD

Q. Chongqing Urban-Rural Infrastructure Development Demonstration II Project

Project No.   :   45509-002 (Proposed)
Amount (US $ million) :   150
Executing Agencies   :   **Chongqing Municipal Government**
Xie Yushan (Ms.), Director Assistant, Chongqing PMO

Sector   :   **Multisector**

Status: Management Review Meeting scheduled on 11 April 2013

Description: Chongqing is one of four centrally-administered municipalities of the People's Republic of China (PRC). Located in the upper middle reaches of the Yangtze River, Chongqing is a part of the less-developed western region which is targeted by the PRC's national preferential policies under the National Strategy for Development of the West (NSDW). Although the NSDW has contributed to double Chongqing's gross domestic product (GDP) in the past five years, economic benefits have been unevenly distributed due to Chongqing's topographical characteristics of vast hinterlands and predominantly hilly and mountainous terrain. In Chongqing, a few rapidly developing central districts co-exist with poverty-stricken peripheral counties, and widening development gaps among districts and counties. Within districts and counties, imbalanced socioeconomic development is also increasingly evident where urban expansion meets rural areas. The urban-rural average income gap increased to 3.4 times in 2010 and 1.45 million people live below the designated poverty line of CNY1,400 per annum. In accordance with the national and municipal strategic priorities, Chongqing has shifted its focus from traditional centralized urban development to balanced urban-rural development. However, many rural villages, small towns and cities still struggle with poor basic infrastructures. In addition to insufficient rural road access and limited water supply provision, frequent flooding in second and third-tier cities becomes a clear development hindrance.

Impact: Improved living standards and quality of life to support balanced urban-rural development in project districts and counties

Outcome: Improved access to safe drinking water and all-weather roads, and resilience to flood risk in project districts and counties

Outputs:
- Rongchang Rongfeng river flood dikes and enhanced landscaping are operating.
- Wulong Wujiang river south bank flood dikes are operating Youyang Longtan river flood dikes are operating Fuling urban-rural road and bridges are opened for traffic.
- Shizhu urban-rural roads and bridges are opened for traffic.
- Wanzhou Yangliu water supply facilities, sludge treatment facilities, pumps and associated operation facilities are operating.

- Project management and capacity building provided to the executing agency and implementing agencies Chengkou urban-rural road and tunnel are opened for traffic

Business Opportunities:
- Consulting Services: In accordance with ADB's Guidelines on the Use of Consultants (2010, as amended from time to time), a consulting firm will be engaged using the quality- and cost-based selection method with a quality:cost ratio of 90:10 using the simplified technical proposal procedure. The terms of reference for the consultant team is subdivided to technical, financial and economic, safeguards and social, and governance teams. The project will engage a total of 13.5 person-months of international position, while a total of 33 person-months for national position.

- Procurement Notices: There are no procurement notices currently available for this project.

Responsible ADB Officer: Satoshi Ishii (E-mail: sishii@adb.org)
East Asia Department
Urban and Social Sectors Division, EARD

R. Guangxi Baise Integrated Urban Environment Rehabilitation
Project No.   :   44022-023 (Proposed)
Amount (US $ million) :   80
Executing Agencies   :   Baise Municipal Government (BMG)
Sector   :   Multisector

Status: Management Review Meeting scheduled on 18 June 2013

Description: The project will directly contribute to poverty reduction by focusing on managing the environmental and social impacts of economic transformation in the city through eliminating highly polluting industries, supporting a new well-regulated industrial zone, and upgrading the living conditions of residents of the old industrial area. The impact of the project is the sustained urban development of Baise towards an environment friendly and livable city. The outcome of the project is a cluster of environment friendly and livable demonstration urban communities developed in Baise City. The project will adopt an integrated urban development approach to produce the following: (i) industrial clean-up and relocation, (ii) ecological restoration and rehabilitation, and (iii) community development and upgrading.

Impact: Sustained urban development of Baise towards an environment friendly and livable city

Outcome: A cluster of environment friendly and livable demonstration urban communities developed in Baise City

Outputs:
1. Clean-up and/or relocation of highly polluting factories from urban residential area for technical upgrading and continued operation in the industrial park
2. Restored and rehabilitated the polluted ecological system and landscape in the project area
3. Urban communities upgraded in the project area

Business Opportunities:
- Consulting Services: All consultants will be recruited according to ADB's Guidelines on the Use of Consultants (2010, as amended from time to time).

- Procurement: All procurement of goods and works will be undertaken in accordance with ADB s Procurement Guidelines (2010, as amended from time to time).

Responsible ADB Officer: Sangay Penjor (E-mail: spenjor@adb.org)
East Asia Department
Urban and Social Sectors Division, EARD

S. Gansu Jiuquan Integrated Urban Environment Improvement Project

Loan No.   **:** **3003**
Project No.   **:** **45506-002**
Amount (US $ million) : **100**
Executing Agencies **:** **Jiuquan Municipal Government**
Sector   **:** **Multisector**

Status: Board approved on 14 June 2013

Description: The project aims to promote environmentally sustainable and socioeconomically inclusive urban development in Jiuquan, Gansu province, by upgrading urban infrastructure and services. The project will support wastewater management, urban transport and utility facilities, windbreak plantation, and related services.

Impact: Environmentally sustainable and socioeconomically inclusive urban development in Jiuquan

Outcome: Improved urban infrastructure and services in Jiuquan

Outputs:
- Wastewater collection and treatment system is operating
- Urban transport and utility facilities are operating
- Windbreak tree screens planted Capacity developed and institutions strengthened

Business Opportunities:
- Consulting Services: Consulting services will be engaged in accordance with ADB's Guidelines on the Use of Consultants (2010, as amended from time to time), whose input requirements and selection method will be determined during project preparation.

- Procurement: All procurement of goods and works will be undertaken in accordance with ADB's Procurement Guidelines (2010, as amended from time to time).

Responsible ADB Officer: Gyongshim An (E-mail: gyongshiman@adb.org)
East Asia Department
Urban and Social Sectors Division, EARD

T. Xinjiang Tacheng Border Cities and Counties Development Project

Project No.   :   46063-002 (Proposed)
Amount (US $ million) :   150
Sector   :   Transport and ICT

Status: Management Review Meeting scheduled on 25 April 2014

Description: The proposed project aims to enhance the living conditions of urban residents of Tacheng City, and of E min, Yumin, and Tuoli counties, in the Xinjiang Uygur Autonomous Region (XUAR), the People's Republic of China (PRC). It is a multisectoral and integrated urban upgrading project that will address urgent infrastructure needs, including: (i) rehabilitation of the Kalangguer urban river corridor and provision of wind-break tree screening; (ii) upgrading of peri-urban areas through construction of urban road and associated utility infrastructure; (iii) provision of new urban infrastructure services to Baktu Liaota New Area (Tacheng City); and (iv) strengthening the institutional capacity for sustainable urban development, planning, and management of Tacheng Municipal Government (TMG).

Impact: Improved living conditions through socially inclusive and environmentally sustainable urbanization in Tacheng City and county cities of E'min, Tuoli, and Yumin

Outcome: Improved urban environmental infrastructure and management services in Tacheng City and county cities of E'min, Tuoli, and Yumin

Outputs:
1. Kalangguer River is rehabilitated.
2. Urban wastewater treatment plant is completed.
3. Urban centralized heating system is upgraded.
4. Urban roads are opened to traffic and associated utility pipeline network and facilities are operating.
5. Institutional capacity is developed and project management support is provided

Business Opportunities:
- Consulting Services: It is expected that the project will finance international and national consulting services to support project implementation, management, and institutional capacity building. These requirements will be determined during project preparatory technical assistance (PPTA) implementation and consulting services will be engaged in accordance with ADB 's Guidelines on the Use of Consultants (2010, as amended from time to time).

- Procurement: All procurement of goods and works will be undertaken in accordance with ADB' s Procurement Guidelines (2010, as amended from time to time). A procurement agent will be hired to support the executing and implementing agencies. Advance contracting and retroactive financing will be considered.

Responsible ADB Officer: Antonio Ressano Garcia (E-mail: aressano@adb.org)
                           East Asia Department
                           Urban and Social Sectors Division, EARD

U. Guangxi Nanning Vocational Education Development

Project No.	:	**46047-002 (Proposed)**
Amount (US $ million)	:	**50**
Sector	:	**Education**

Status: Management Review Meeting scheduled on 2 August 2013

Description: The proposed project will help improve the capacity and effectiveness of social services focused technical and vocational education and training (TVET) in Nanning. It will support improvement of No. 4 Vocational Secondary School and Nanning Health School, thereby creating a cadre of qualified kindergarten teachers and nurses to address current skilled worker shortages and inadequate extension of social services. The proposed project will be only the second Asian Development Bank (ADB)-financed TVET investment project in the People s Republic of China (PRC), and will play a demonstration role for the sector and provinces seeking to provide quality public social services.

Impact: Improved delivery of public social services (preschool, health) in Nanning

Outcome: Improved human resources and capacity of TVET in Nanning No. 4 Vocational School and Nanning Health School

Outputs: Upgraded facilities Upgraded equipment Capacity strengthened and demonstration pilots on TVET implemented

Business Opportunities:
- Consulting Services: The consulting services will be engaged by ADB, in accordance with ADB Guidelines on the Use of Consultants (2010, as amended from time to time), to ensure immediate mobilization to facilitate project scoping. ADB will select and engage an international firm based on the quality of the proposal (80%) and the cost (20%) of the services to be provided (the quality- and cost-based selection method, QCBS) using the simplified technical proposal procedure. A total of 54 person-months of consulting services (18 international and 36 national) are required. The firm will provide expertise in TVET, labor market analysis, competency-based curriculum, services-school collaboration, training of instructors, management of TVET, finance and economics, engineering, poverty and social assessment and development, resettlement, environment, institutional development, and project management.

- Procurement Notices: To be determined

Responsible ADB Officer: Wendy M. Walker (E-mail: wwalker@adb.org)
East Asia Department
Urban and Social Sectors Division, EARD

V. Hunan Technical and Vocational Education and Training Demonstration Project

Loan No.   :   3010
Project No.   :   45511-006
Amount (US $ million) :   50
Executing Agencies   :   Hunan Provincial Government
Sector   :   Education

Status: Board approved on 28 June 2013.

Description: The project will provide targeted support to 13 public technical and vocational education and training (TVET) institutions in Hunan to strengthen the capability to deliver demand-driven quality programs related to priority industries. The project will: (i) build capacity of the industry advisory groups (IAGs) and foster partnerships between 13 project TVET institutions and employers to jointly develop the skills needed at the work place, and prepare graduates who are able to adjust to changing demands in the labor market quickly; (ii) modernize the curriculum by developing competency-based curriculum in priority areas, (iii) upgrade instructional capacity of vocational instructors; (iv) build management capacity in strategic planning, monitoring key performance indicators, and linkages with the industry; (v) pilot a labor market information system to identify priority skills areas and to adjust TVET programs to meet the skill requirements of Hunan's workforce; (vi) develop institutional partnerships between selected project TVET institutions and overseas vocational colleges for international benchmarking, student and faculty exchange, joint curriculum revision, and to foster a learning culture in the project TVET institutions through twinning arrangements; and (vii) upgrade equipment and facilities in selected TVET institutions. The project will set up curriculum development committees with industry representation to develop modular curricula and a TVET review committee with qualified industry experts to validate the curriculum and other project outputs, and to ensure the curriculum meets identified industry needs. Training equipment will be approved by relevant IAGs. Strategic fit. The project is the first Asian Development Bank (ADB)-financed lending project for TVET in the People's Republic of China (PRC) and is envisaged to play a demonstration role for TVET development in the country. Because worker skills and education are viewed as a constraint to the PRC s inclusive growth, ADB involvement in the TVET sector is strongly justified. The project supports ADB s education policy and education sector strategies and Strategy 2020: The Long-Term Strategic Framework of the Asian Development Bank 2008- 2020 . It aligns with the ADB s PRC country partnership strategy (2011- 2015) and supports the PRC s 12th Five-Year Plan, which prioritizes developing high-quality human resources, increasing scientific and technological innovations, and accelerating educational reform. The project has the following demonstration features for replication in other provinces of the PRC: (i) Industry involvement. The project will strengthen partnerships between TVET institutions and industries, and build capacity of sector-specific IAGs in the priority sectors; (ii) Promoting inclusive TVET through information communication technology. The project will broaden access for students from remote areas by developing online TVET courses and thus, will foster sharing of teaching and learning resources among well-developed TVET institutions in urban areas and disadvantaged TVET institutions in poor and remote areas to benefit students in project and non-project TVET institutions; and (iii) Greening TVET provision. The project will contribute to the PRC Government s objectives of developing an environmentally sustainable and energy-efficient society under its 12th Five-Year Plan by designing, constructing, and maintaining teaching and learning buildings that reduce energy and water use and promoting sustainable practices such as reducing, reusing, and recycling resources; encouraging selection of training equipment with low energy consumption; and skills mapping to identify skills needed for environmentally sustainable development in Hunan. Incorporation of the lessons learned. Lessons from activities in skills training supported by ADB and the World Bank were incorporated into the project design. The lessons learned include (i) actively involving representatives of industries and IAGs in identifying occupational areas that are in demand, developing competencies for the market-demanded occupational areas, and working with the project TVET institutions to develop modular, competency-based curricula and learning materials; (ii) conducting tracer studies of the trainees, and strengthening the capacity of the relevant government agencies and the TVET institutions to analyze labor market demand; and (iii) establishing a project benefit monitoring and evaluation system.

Impact: Skilled human resources contribute to inclusive growth and social development in Hunan province

Outcome: Strengthened capacity of the TVET system to meet labor market needs

Outputs:
1. Improved quality and management of TVET system
2. Upgraded facilities and learning environments
3. Strengthened industry involvement in TVET
4. Project management support established

Business Opportunities:
- Consulting Services: All consultants will be recruited according to ADB's Guidelines on the Use of Consultants.

- Procurement: All procurement of goods and works will be undertaken in accordance with the Asian Development Bank's (ADB) Procurement Guidelines.

Responsible ADB Officer: Jazira Asanova (E-mail: jasanova@adb.org)
East Asia Department
Urban and Social Sectors Division, EARD

W. Gansu Jinta Concentrated Solar Power Project

Project No.	:	**47006-002 (Proposed)**
Amount (US $ million)	:	**100**
Executing Agencies	:	**China Huadian Corp.**
Sector	:	**Energy**

Status: Management Review Meeting on 20 September 2013

Impact: Expanded share of CSP plants in the renewable energy mix in the PRC

Outcome: Demonstrated feasibility of a utility scale CSP plant

Outputs:
- Construct a 50 MW CSP plant with thermal storage including a natural gas back-up system in Gansu Province.
- Capacity development and training in CSP design, procurement, construction, and operation and management for technical risks assessment and mitigation measures.

Business Opportunities
- Procurement: To be determined

- Consulting services: To be determined

Responsible ADB Officer: Woo Lee (E-mail: wylee@adb.org)
East Asia Department
Energy Division, EARD

INDIA

A. West Bengal North-South Corridor Project (formerly West Bengal Haldia Port Connectivity Project)

Project No.   :   45265-001 (Proposed)
Amount (US $ million) :   300
Executing Agencies   :   West Bengal Public Works (Roads) Department
Sector   :   Transport and ICT

Status: Proposed; management review meeting scheduled on March 3, 2014

Description: The West Bengal Port Connectivity Project (the Project) will widen about 270 km of state highways in the state of West Bengal, India and strengthen the capacity of the West Bengal Public Works (Roads) Department (PWRD) to efficiently develop, operate and maintain state highway network. Consulting services will be provided to supervise the implementation of civil works. A Technical Assistance (TA) will be provided to modernize PWRD in terms of institutional development and private sector participation, with focus on overload control.

Project Rationale and Linkage to Country/Regional Strategy: The State of West Bengal is on the threshold of a new era of industrialization. One of the major infrastructural requirements of industry is proper road connectivity. The general condition of roads in West Bengal is not satisfactory and per capita road length is much below the country average. The vehicle population in the state has been increasing at an average of more than 10 percent; the rate of traffic growth is expected to rise along with increasing industrialization and development activities in the coming years. Therefore widening, strengthening, and upgrading of the road network, which is suffering from capacity and strength constraints, have become urgently necessary. Among the state road network, the connectivity with Haldia port is significantly important not only for the overall state economy but also subregional economy. The improved port connectivity will remove a critical bottleneck in the movement of freight and passengers not only from the northern parts of West Bengal and the northeastern states of India, but also neighboring landlocked counties, e.g., Bhutan and Nepal, to Haldia port. The Project provides alternative route to SAARC Highway Corridors 2 and 3. The proposed north-south corridor comprising State Highways 4 and 7 passes through the trunk backbone of West Bengal along districts with high poverty but with abundance of agricultural products. The development of this route will also maximize the effect of infrastructural development, economic growth and poverty reduction in this area. The Project will develop economy of project areas as well as provide neighboring countries with an alternative link to Haldia port for regional and global markets. Connectivity through improved transport has important implications for poverty reduction by offering new economic opportunities through better market linkages and increased employment possibilities. The Project is relevant to achieving results of the Country Strategy and Program (2009-2012), supporting regional cooperation and more port and intermodal connectivity; as well as the draft Regional Cooperation Strategy and Programs (2011-2015), improving South Asia subregional connectivity and facilitating intraregional trade in South Asia. The Project is included in the draft Country Operation Business Plan (2012-2014).

Impact: Improved the north-south connectivity of the state road network, including connection with the Haldia Port

Outcome: Efficient, reliable and safe road transport in West Bengal

Outputs:
1. Widened state roads
2. Improved capacities for overloading control
3. Improved capacity for road development and maintenance

Business Opportunities
- Consulting Services: International consulting firms and/or national consultants will be recruited for construction consultant supervision in accordance with ADB's Guidelines on the Use of Consultants (2007, as amended from time to time). Advance contracting will be undertaken to enhance project readiness.
- Procurement to be financed from the ADB loan will be undertaken in accordance with ADB's Procurement Guidelines (2007, as amended from time to time). Advance contracting is proposed to ensure the project readiness. Contract packaging will be firmed up during project processing.

Responsible ADB Officer: Hiroaki Yamaguchi (E-mail: hyamaguchi@adb.org)
South Asia Department
Transport and Communications Division, SARD

B. Meghalaya Public Management Reform Program

Project No.	:	**42262-013 (Proposed)**
Amount (US $ million)	:	**100**
Executing Agencies	:	**Finance Department**
Sector	:	**Public sector management**

Status: Proposed; management review meeting scheduled on June 8, 2011

Project Rationale and Linkage to Country/Regional Strategy: The proposed Meghalaya Public Resource Management Development Program (MPRMDP, the Program) will be designed to assist the Government of Meghalaya (GoM) to improve service delivery, while keeping the state to a sustainable fiscal consolidation path consistent with the state's overall fiscal target. Moreover, the Program will be aligned to the outcomes sought by GoM and the Government of India (GOI), and will draw heavily on the lessons learned from similar programs in India. Meghalaya is a special category state with a rather weak economic base, and development infrastructure and endowments in the state are rather limited. Difficult geographical terrain has meant difficulties not only in water shortages, but also agriculture backwardness (in farming systems and agricultural productivity), transportation, communication, etc. Consequently, there is a strong dependency on resource transfers from the central government and a limited scope for mobilizing the state's own resources for providing and sustaining improved service delivery. Thus, the logic of the proposed Program is based on the link between creation of fiscal space as a means to complement central transfers and build up and maintain social service improvements in the key areas and thereby contribute to improving social welfare and minimizing human and social poverty. The Program lending modality is preferred because the proposed Program will require adjustments to policies and investment plans, and complimentary capacity building of institutions.

Impact: Improved social and gender-inclusive human development parameters in the state

Outcome: Creating greater fiscal space for meeting the state's development financing requirements
Implementation Progress

Outputs:
1. The management of public expenditure is rationalized.
2. Tax and nontax revenue reforms successfully implemented
3. State government debts are effectively restructured and managed.
4. Services in the health and education sectors are more accessible and improved.

Business Opportunities
- Consulting Services: To be determined

- Procurement: To be determined

Responsible ADB Officer: Shamit Chakravarti (E-mail: schakravarti@adb.org)
South Asia Department
Human and Social Development Division, SARD

C. Catalyzing Sustainable Finance Facility

Project No.   :   **44452-014 (Proposed)**
Amount (US $ million) :   150
Sector   :   **Finance**

Status: Proposed; management review meeting scheduled on June 11, 2014

Description: The Facility is an innovative leveraged finance mechanism designed as a financial intermediation loan with linked conditions for on lending to subprojects in challenging urban infrastructure sectors. Eligible subprojects are those in the following sub-sectors:
-Affordable housing in urban areas;
-Housing for economically weaker sections in urban and rural areas;
-Slum rehabilitation including provision of basic services in slums, provision of temporary and transit shelters for poor.
-Basic urban services, including water supply, sewerage, drainage, solid waste management, sanitation, and other physical infrastructure in urban areas; and
-Projects fostering community involvement and inclusion, such as community based tourism. The proposed CSF Facility is a concept developed between HUDCO and ADB, which utilizes ADB's financial intermediation (FI) loan modality. It aims to create financing avenues in challenging urban sectors with a high developmental impact, and doing so through a commercially sustainable structure. With a pipeline of projects emerging in sectors that have been traditionally regarded as challenging, there is now a need for a financing source that can be used to support such projects. Such finance, linked to bankability and sustainability reforms, would attract commercial financing to these projects. The CSF is thus positioned as a quick disbursing fund managed by HUDCO. The CSF Facility will also link into the project development that is already underway under the GOI-ADB PPP Initiative to ensure that projects are upfront financing assistance to graduate to bankability status. The Housing and Urban Development Corporation (HUDCO) is the selected financial intermediary (FI), which, under oversight of the Ministry of Housing and Urban Poverty Alleviation, will manage the facility per tightly defined selection and bankability assurance parameters. The project therefore follows a 'finance plus' approach, directly congruent with ADB's strategy for India, which emphasizes infrastructure development and serves to leverage ADB resources for the benefit of the client country.

Project Rationale and Linkage to Country/Regional Strategy: Infrastructure financing requirements in India are escalating and need a diversified source of funds. Investment needs, critical for sustained economic growth, estimated at $1 trillion in the 12th Five Year Plan approach paper (2012-2017) of the Planning Commission of India, are already beyond public sector capacities alone. The 11th Five Year Plan estimates around 36% private sector contribution to infrastructure investment to date and this is projected to reach 50% and above under the 12th Five Year Plan. The Government of India (GOI) is thus focusing on catalyzing commercial and private sector funds including public-private partnerships to meet this gap, and has developed several PPP enabling frameworks including the: (i) viability gap fund (VGF) (grant fund), (ii) India Infrastructure Finance Company Limited (IIFCL), (iii) India Infrastructure Project Development Fund (IIPDF), and (iv) a host of other initiatives at the central government and state government levels. The Facility links with the ongoing ADB-GOI PPP Initiative for project pipelines and structuring assistance. It furthers the existing GOI tools, VGF, and IIFCL. These tools have mostly funded road and power projects, which can be made viable through VGF, or are viable on a stand-alone basis (through IIFCL). Hence, the existing tools are not likely to enable commercial finance in sectors targeted by the Facility which have a significant viability gap. By providing substantial support in eligible sector subprojects, the Facility thus directly enables partial commercial or private sector finance to further flow. Thus, the project directly supports GOI priorities for a 'finance plus' approach per the India Country Programming Mission 2011, which refers to the improved leveraging of ADB finance, catalyzing private finance, piloting innovation and sustainability, and sector reforms, all of which the Facility is designed to address.

Impact: Expanded coverage and service delivery of infrastructure in the eligible subsectors

Outcome: A greater flow of commercial and/or private sector financing into eligible subsectors and service delivery management, through replication of bankability and sector frameworks.

Outputs:
- Creation of ring-fenced institutional structures for better implementation and governance of infrastructure projects and services in eligible subsectors
- Creation of bankable financial models and capital structures for attracting commercial and/or private sector finance in eligible subsectors
- Replication of the CSF leveraged finance funding facility with systems and linked reform conditions for outreach to eligible subsectors

Business Opportunities
- Consulting Services: To be determined

- Procurement: To be determined

Responsible ADB Officer: Peter Marro (E-mail: pmarro@adb.org)
South Asia Department
Public Management, Financial Sector and Trade Division, SARD

D. Punjab Development Finance Program

Project No.	:	**45288-002 (Proposed)**
Amount (US $ million)	:	**200.4**
Executing Agencies	:	**Finance Department, Government of Punjab**
Sector	:	**Public sector management**

Status: Management review meeting scheduled on 15 July 2013

Project Rationale and Linkage to Country/Regional Strategy: The proposed program seeks to facilitate implementation of a comprehensive fiscal consolidation program in Punjab. This will generate fiscal savings and thereby assist Punjab to augment and sustain growth enhancing development financing. Punjab is primarily an agrarian economy with a population of 28 million. Punjab has always been instrumental in ensuring national food security since 1960s. The Government of Punjab (GOP) traditionally provides various subsidies, including free power to farmers, to promote agriculture in the state. Despite these schemes, Punjab agriculture is currently constrained by declining productivity, soil degradation, and water depletion. Despite relatively robust own-tax effort in Punjab with an own-tax to gross state domestic product (GSDP) ratio of 8.2%, Punjab's extremely fragile fiscal situation could primarily be attributed to ad hoc expenditure planning and management with untargeted transfer payment and subsidy schemes. The deteriorating fiscal situation in Punjab has placed added pressures on public resources constraining development financing (investment), leading to poor delivery of public goods and services in the state. The committed expenditures of the state government (those on salaries, pensions, interest payments, and subsidies alone) have almost exhausted the total revenue receipts of the state in recent years, requiring the state to undertake even larger borrowings to finance these expenditures, thereby trapping the state in a vicious cycle of mounting current account (revenue) and fiscal deficits. The committed liabilities, including subsidies, were almost 100% of revenue receipts during the 11th plan period (2007-2012). The weak financial performance of the public sector enterprises (PSEs) including newly created Punjab State Power Corporation Limited (PSPCL) and Punjab State Transmission Corporation Limited (PSTCL) has further exacerbated the growing fiscal imbalances and mounting public debt. A major contributory factor to fiscal distress is the state's poor expenditure planning and management tradition. GOP does not follow the system of project appraisal before approving a project. Moreover, the lack of evaluation and monitoring system causes inordinate delays in project execution, leading to escalation in costs and the projects, quite often, fail to deliver the desired outcomes. More importantly, untargeted power subsidy, triggered by populist policies, has brought both the state exchequer and the power sector on the brink of financial collapse. This has many implications. First, PSPCL is unable to modernize the power infrastructure due to lack of borrowing opportunities from the banks and financial institutions. Second, the deteriorating fiscal situation of GOP has had negative consequences for GOP's development agenda. In particular, the increase in nondiscretionary committed expenditure has reduced fiscal space limiting the ability of GOP to make effective use of public spending to meet its policy priorities. More directly, this has resulted in a large opportunity cost as the disproportionate share of the fiscal adjustment fell on capital spending.

Impact: Improved and sustainable development financing in the state

Outcome: Greater and sustainable fiscal space is achieved in the GOP budget

Outputs:
1. Improved expenditure efficiency
2. Improved tax and nontax revenue efforts
3. Efficient debt management
4. Selected PSEs restructured

Business Opportunities
- Consulting Services: To be determined

- Procurement: To be determined

Responsible ADB Officer: Hiranya Mukhopadhyay (E-mail: hmukhopadhyay@adb.org)
South Asia Department
Public Management, Financial Sector and Trade Division, SARD

E. Supporting Human Capital Development in Meghalaya

Project No.   :   46166-001 (Proposed)
Amount (US $ million) :   100
Executing Agencies   :   Finance Department
Sector   :   Public sector management

Status: Fact-finding scheduled on November 12 - 19, 2012

Description: The proposed project will help in enhancing the employability of Meghalaya's youth by improving the quality and delivery of its skill development and secondary education programs.

Impact: Improved human capital in Meghalaya.

Outcome: Facilitating environment created for improving Meghalaya's human capital

Outputs:
1. Meghalaya's Skill Development Mission operationalized
2. Improved learning environment in secondary schools
3. Strengthened capacity in relevant Departments
4. Project management system in place.

Business Opportunities
- Consulting Services: For the small scale project preparatory technical assistance (PPTA), ADB will engage a firm in accordance with the Guidelines on the Use of Consultants (2010, as amended). The consultant qualification selection (CQS) method based on a review of bio-data technical proposal will be used since the processing schedule is tight, and the size of the consulting package is less than $200,000. 1 international consultant for a total of 2 person months and 9 national consultants for a total 16 person months will be required. Two individual consultants (civil engineer / architect) will be hired for 1.5 months each to expedite the survey of buildings. The total consulting requirement is 12 consultants for 21 person months in all.

- Procurement: To be determined

Responsible ADB Officer: Hiranya Mukhopadhyay (E-mail: hmukhopadhyay@adb.org)
                             South Asia Department
                             Public Management, Financial Sector and Trade Division, SARD

F. Himachal Pradesh Clean Energy Transmission Investment Program - Tranche 2

Loan No.   :   3001
Project No.   :   43464-026
Amount (US $ million) :   110
Executing Agencies :   Himachal Pradesh Power Transmission Corp. Ltd.
Sector   :   Energy

Status: Board Approval scheduled on 7 May 2013

Description: The project consists of:

1. New Transmission System Assets
A. Transmission Line Construction - i. 33 kV D/C line from 33 kV Palchan switching station to 33/220 kV substation in the yard of Allain Dhuangan HEP; ii. 66 kV D/C Line from 66 kV Switching station at Urni to Wangtoo Substation; iii. 220 kV Line from 33/220 kV Lahal substation up to 220 kV Yard of Budhil HEP. iv. 220 kV D/C (Twin MOOSE) Transmission Line from Sunda to Hatkoti. v. 132 kV S/C line on D/C towers form Banjal to Kurthala. vi. 220 kV D/C line (Twin MOOSE) from Charor to 400/220 kV Banala substation of PGCIL. vii. 132 kV D/C line from Barsaini to Charor.

B. Construction of Sub Stations - i. 33 kV Switching station at Palchan. ii. 66 kV Switching station at Urni. iii. 33/220 kV, 50/63 MVA P.S at Lahal, iv. 220 kV Switching Station at Hatkoti, v. 132/220 kV, 2x100 MVA Pooling Station at Sunda, vi. 33/132, 2x25/31.5 MVA substation at Chambi (Shahpur) with LILO of 132 kV Kangra-Dehra S/C Line, vii. 33/132 kV substation at Pandoh+LILO of one circuit of 132 kV Bajaura-Kangoo D/C Line, viii. 33/132 kV, 1x50/63 MVA sub station Banjal, ix. 33/132 kV, 1x31.5 MVA substation at Barsaini, x. 132/220 kV, 1x80/100 MVA Sub Station at Charor.

2. Capacity Development
i. Computerized enterprise resource planning solution design and installation phase II.
ii. Additional computer equipment
iii. Training program.

Impact: Increased electricity transmission in Himachal Pradesh

Outcome: Improved capacity of HPPTCL to transmit electricity from hydropower generation sources within and outside of Himachal Pradesh.

Outputs: New Transmission system assets are operational Enterprise resource planning (ERP) system, phase II and additional IT hardware installed in HPPTCL corporate facilities and are operational Capacity of HPPTCL personnel on project management, and transmission utility operations improved

Business Opportunities:
- Procurement: To be determined

- Consulting Services: To be determined

Responsible ADB Officer: Andrew Jeffries (E-mail: ajeffries@adb.org)
South Asia Department
Energy Division, SARD

KYRGYZ

CAREC Corridor 3 (Bishkek-Osh Road) Improvement Project, Phase 4

Project No.	:	**45169-001 (Proposed)**
Amount (US $ million)	:	**100**
Executing Agencies	:	**Ministry of Transportation and Communications**
Sector	:	**Transport and ICT**

Status: Proposed; management review meeting scheduled on August 9, 2013

Description: The proposed CAREC Corridor 3 (Bishkek-Osh Road) Improvement Project, Phase 4 (the project) will improve the national and regional connectivity by rehabilitating an estimated 130 kilometers (km) of crucial road sections between Bishkek and Osh. The impact of the proposed project will be improved connectivity and access to markets. The outcome of the project will be efficient movement of freight and passenger traffic along the Bishkek-Osh road. The project outputs will be: (i) 60 km of rehabilitated road from Bishkek to Kara Balta, (ii) 70 km of rehabilitated road from Madaniyak to Jalalabad, (iii) strengthened road asset management system, and (iv) improved road safety.

Project Rationale and Linkage to Country/Regional Strategy: The Asian Development Bank (ADB) has assisted the Kyrgyz Republic in rehabilitating 483 km of the 655 km Bishkek-Osh road through three loans in a total amount of $140 million. Other development partners cofinanced the rehabilitation of this road. Combined, the development partners have assisted the government in rehabilitating over 539 km (82%) of the Bishkek-Osh road. However, due to funding limitations, there remain two missing sections of the Bishkek-Osh road needing rehabilitation: Bishkek to Kara Balta (60 km) and Madaniyak to Jalalabad (70 km). The state of these roads warrants urgent attention. Road improvement in the adjacent sections attracts increased traffic, but the two sections will not be able to provide the needed level of service and will also pose traffic hazards. Therefore, the government has requested ADB to help rehabilitate the two road sections under the project.

Impact: Improved connectivity and access to markets

Outcome: Efficient movement of freight and passenger traffic along the Bishkek-Osh road

Outputs:
- 60km of rehabilitated road from Bishkek to Kara Balta
- 70 km of rehabilitated road from Madaniyak to Jalalabad
- Strengthened Road asset management system
- Improved road safety

Responsible ADB Officer: Susan Lim (E-mail: slim@adb.org)
Central and West Asia Department
Transport and Communications Division, CWRD

NEPAL

A. Bagmati River Basin Improvement Project

Project No.   :   43448-013 (Proposed)
Amount (US $ million) :   30
Sector   :   Multisector

Status: Fact-finding scheduled on April 16 – 26, 2013

Description: The Bagmati River Basin Improvement Project aims to improve water security and resilience to potential climate change impact in the Bagmati River Basin. It will build on the general public's desire to restore the river environment in the Kathmandu Valley and the Government's efforts to improve irrigation development and mitigate the impact of water-induced disasters in the middle and lower reaches of the basin. The Project adopts the principles of integrated water resources management (IWRM) and provides Nepal with its first opportunity to apply this key policy element since it has been adopted under the national water plan in 2005. The Project's expected impact is to improve sustainable economic development and poverty reduction in the Bagmati River Basin. The Project outcome will focus on improving water security in the Bagmati River Basin. The expected outputs may include: (i) effective integrated and participatory river basin management, (ii) an integrated river basin development master plan and action plan agreed by all stakeholders, (iii) an improved riparian river environment in the Kathmandu Valley, (iv) increased water availability in the basin during the dry season, and (v) reduced water-induced disaster impact on the basin communities. The major investment components may include: (i) stakeholder mobilization, awareness raising and integrated planning; (ii) IWRM focused institutional reform and capacity building; (iii) riparian river environment improvement that may include community/civil society based: (a) awareness and education, (b) river training works, (c) river cleaning, (d) river side beautification including cultural heritage sites restoration; (iii) increased surface water availability (rain water harvesting and storage, catchment regeneration, irrigation rehabilitation and efficiency and natural wetland enhancement); and (iv) water-induced disaster mitigation that may include (a) river training works, (b) watershed regeneration, (c) sabo works, and (d) community-based flood early warning systems and adaptation programs. A project preparatory technical assistance (PPTA) will assess the detailed cost per component for the Project.

Impact: Economic development sustained and poverty reduced in the Bagmati River Basin

Outcome: Bagmati River Basin water security is improved.

Outputs:
- Effective integrated and participatory river basin management made operational
- Improved riparian river environment in the Kathmandu Valley
- Increased water availability in the basin during dry season
- Efficient project management and stakeholders coordination is achieved
- Reduced water-induced disaster impact on basin communities

Business Opportunities
- Consulting Services: To be determined

- Procurement: To be determined

Responsible ADB Officer: Arnaud M. Cauchois (E-mail: acauchois@adb.org)
                                     South Asia Department
                                     Environment, Natural Resources & Agriculture Division, SARD

B. Rural Electrification through Renewable Energy

Project No.	:	**45126-003 (Proposed)**
Amount (US $ million)	:	**20.8**
Executing Agencies	:	**Ministry of Environment**
Sector	:	**Energy**

Status: Proposed; fact-finding scheduled on Jan 23 to 30, 2013

Description: The proposed Project aims to address these constraints by leveraging Strategic Climate Fund (SCF) funds with ADB and other donor-assisted funds to set up both credit and subsidy windows for mini-micro hydropower (MMH) and solar home systems (SHS) under Central Renewable Energy Fund (CREF). Funds under the CREF will be managed by a nodal financial intermediary (FI) for relending of medium to long-term local currency subloans and providing other support to participating financial institutions (PFIs) that meet ADB's eligibility criteria to help finance the development of off-grid MMH and SHS subprojects.

Impact: Scaling up of renewable energy development in Nepal

Outcome: Enhanced credit and subsidies delivery mechanisms for development of mini-micro hydropower (MMH) and solar home systems (SHS)

Outputs:
1. The credit and subsidy fund windows for mini-micro hydropower (MMH) and solar home system (SHS) under the CREF developed.
2. Capacities of the EA/IA and FI/PFIs on RE technologies, project appraisals, financing mechanisms and overall effective operation of CREF developed.

Business Opportunities
- Consulting Services: To be determined

- Procurement: To be determined

Responsible ADB Officer: Zhang Lei (E-mail: zlei@adb.org)
South Asia Department
Energy Division, SARD

PAKISTAN

A. Power Sector Rehabilitation Project

Project No.   :   46218-001 (Proposed)
Amount (US $ million) :   433
Executing Agencies :   GENCO Holding Company Limited
Sector   :   Multisector

Status: Proposed; management review meeting scheduled on October 4, 2012

Description: Jamshoro Thermal Power Plant (TPP) and Guddu TPP will have: (i) equipment replacement, (ii) major overhauls, and (iii) spare parts provision. 400 MW power output will be recovered. Two 200 MW oil/gas-fueled boilers of Jamshoro TPP will be replaced and converted to a 400 MW subcritical coal-fired boiler. The project will include coal and ash handling systems and modification/improvements of other auxiliary equipment. This conversion to subcritical coal-fired system is the least-cost method which will also diversify the fuel mix away from imported fuel oil. ADB's Energy Policy (2009) supports such diversification which will improve power system reliability and energy security, and the least-cost option. Efficiency improvement of 3% to 8% and net environmental benefits from greenhouse gas (GHG) reduction are also expected. The plants will adhere to national environmental standards.

Project Rationale and Linkage to Country/Regional Strategy: The Power Sector Rehabilitation Project (the Project) will rehabilitate government-owned thermal power generation plants (GENCO plants) to recover de-rated capacity and to increase reliable power output by 400-700 megawatts (MW) through improved efficiency. The project will cover two power plants in Sindh. The persistent energy shortage which in FY2011 reached a peak of 5,000 MW represents around 30% of total demand. This has made life difficult for all Pakistanis. Many urban areas are experiencing power interruptions beyond 10 hours a day; some rural areas double that figure. The manufacturing sector, especially small- and medium-sized enterprises that usually cannot afford back-up generators, is the hardest hit. Estimates from the Planning Commission suggest that losses arising from power and gas shortages reduced gross domestic product (GDP) growth by 3% - 4% in both FY2011 and FY2012. The ongoing energy crisis can be diagnosed through three pillars: (i) domestic power generation capacity not keeping up with demand, (ii) financial issues, and (iii) management issues. With Pakistan's ongoing reforms following the recommendations in the Friends of Democratic Pakistan Energy Task Force Report, progress is being made to diversify fuel sources, lower costs, and move towards cost recovery tariff. To improve power sector management and resolve financing issues, Asian Development Bank (ADB) continues to support the government as the largest donor in the sector and address project specific-issues through project design. The Project addresses the first and second pillars by increasing the power produced by the existing power plants and decreasing costs per kilowatt hour.

Responsible ADB Officer: F. Cleo Kawawaki (E-mail: fkawawaki@adb.org)
                        Central and West Asia Department
                        Energy Division, CWRD

PHILIPPINES

A. Solid Waste Management Sector Project

Project No.	:	**45146-002 (Proposed)**
Amount (US $ million)	:	**70**
Sector	:	**Waste Management**

Status: Management Review Meeting scheduled on 26 Oct 2012

Impact: Improved public health in participating LGUs

Outcome: Efficient management of solid waste by the participating LGUs

Outputs:
- Solid waste management plans at LGU levels prepared
- Investment programs for solid waste management facilities completed
- Project management and institutional capacity improved

Business Opportunities
- Consulting Services: To be determined

- Procurement: To be determined

Responsible ADB Officer: Rudolf Frauendorfer (E-mail: rfrauendorfer@adb.org)
Southeast Asia Department
Urban Development and Water Division, SERD

B. Urban Water Supply and Sanitation Project

Project No.	:	**42363-013 (Proposed)**
Amount (US $ million)	:	**70**
Executing Agencies	:	**Metro Cebu Water District**
		Davao City Water District
Sector	:	**Water Supply and Sanitation (WSS)**

Status: Management Review Meeting scheduled on 15 April 2013

Description: The Urban Water Supply and Sanitation Project aims to improve the WSS services in Metro Cebu, Davao City and other to be identified urban areas, by providing investment capital and technical assistance to the respective Water Districts (WDs). Of the population in the water districts mandated service area by 2022, at least 80% will have access to potable water supply and 50% will have access to safe sanitation and will adopt proper hygiene practices. This outcome will be achieved by closing of the Project through five main outputs: (i) Raw water supply capacity expanded. Primary focus will be on the reduction of physical leakage component of non-revenue water in order to make higher quantities of water available to customers. In addition, new bulk water sources need to be developed from surface water sources or through desalination. Climate change mitigation measures will be identified to ensure sustainability of source capacity; (ii) Water supply distribution systems rehabilitated and expanded. Currently the distribution systems cover a limited area and need to be expanded, while existing systems need urgent replacement. Also, the distribution systems consist of various independent systems which may need to be connected. Additional sources may lead to the requirement to re-align the system; (iii) Awareness of the benefits of sanitation services increased. The communities should be made aware of the health and financial benefits of hygienic sanitation, leading to demand for the services. Similarly, policy and decision makers should be made aware of the economic benefits of sanitation and waste water management. This can be achieved through extensive public promotion campaigns, supported through the development of a sanitation strategy: to initiate dialogue between and create support from various stakeholders; and pilot projects: to demonstrate the effectiveness of sanitation services; (iv) Constructed and operational waste water collection, treatment and disposal facilities. High priority investments will be identified, developed, constructed and operated. The preparation phase should outline the requirements regarding: capacity development, financial resources, and revenue collection mechanism. Following construction, aftercare is to be provided through continuous training and management assistance, including continuation of awareness campaigns to ensure sustainability of the infrastructure. (v) Operational sanitation strategy.

The sanitation strategy should: (i) cover on-site sanitation, sewerage discharge and treatment, and drainage; (ii) be an issue based, dynamic framework for 5-year investment plans, to be reviewed and updated every 2 to 3 years; (iii) identify the development issues, relevant parameters and monitoring mechanisms required to update the plan, such as demographic development, planned government investments, private investments, etc; and (iv) have a hygiene educational program and investment plan attached. The investment needs for water supply and waste water management until 2022 for DCWD and MCWD combined, are estimated to be $800 million. These investments will be financed by combination of public and private debt, and equity.

Project Rationale and Linkage to Country/Regional Strategy: The foreseen impact of the Project is a reduction of the occurrence of water related health diseases in the mandated service areas of MCWD and DCWD. Indicative data shows that diarrheal diseases in Davao City and Metro Cebu have a higher prevalence in the more urbanized areas, with morbidity rates varying from 200 to 1,200 cases per 100,000 populations, and reaching as high as 3,500 cases, and mortality rates as high as 14 cases per 100,000 populations. The data also show that in all cities 70% of the cases occur with children younger than 5 years.

Impact: Reduced occurrence of water-borne and water washed diseases in the water districts' service areas.

Outcome: Increased access to water supply and sanitation services

Business Opportunities
- Consulting Services: To be determined

- Procurement: To be determined

Responsible ADB Officer: Paulus B. van Klaveren (E-mail: pvanklaveren@adb.org)
Southeast Asia Department
Urban Development and Water Division, SERD

C. Angat Water Transmission Improvement Project

Project No.   :   46362-002 (Proposed)
Amount (US $ million) :   50
Sector   :   **Water Supply and Sanitation**

Status: Management Review Meeting on 19 July 2013

Description: The Project will secure raw water supply to the 13 million inhabitants of Metropolitan Waterworks and Sewerage System (MWSS) service area, through the rehabilitation of the Angat transmission line. It is estimated that currently each day about 800,000 cubic meter (m^3) or 20% of the total potential capacity of raw water is lost due to leakage of the aqueducts. The main components of the Angat transmission line are as old as 50 years, in poor condition, and not in compliance with structural and seismic requirements, risking the partial interruption of Metro Manila s water supply. The proposed financing modality is a Project loan.

Project Rationale and Linkage to Country/Regional Strategy: Provision of water supply and sanitation in Metro Manila (Manila) is the responsibility of MWSS, a government-owned corporation. In 1997, it awarded two concession contracts to private firms for water distribution. MWSS retained responsibility for bulk water supply. The privatization of the distribution services brought about significant improvements in the delivery of water supply services. The serviced population has doubled since 1997, of which more than 90% have 24 hours access. The nonrevenue water level (NRW) of over 60% in 2002 currently ranges from 10 to 40%. MWSS's capacity to fulfill its responsibility of ensuring and securing the availability of raw water to the concessionaries needs to be strengthened by: (i) rehabilitation of the raw water transmission system; and (ii) adopting a comprehensive water safety, risk- and asset management system.

Impact: Sustained and secured water supply from the Angat reservoir

Outcome: Sustainable operation of aqueducts

Outputs:
   ▪   Most urgent aqueduct rehabilitation and/or construction works implemented
   ▪   Water safety, risk and asset management plans are operational

Business Opportunities
   ▪   Consulting Services: To be determined

   ▪   Procurement: To be determined

Responsible ADB Officer: Paulus B. van Klaveren (E-mail: pvanklaveren@adb.org)
                          Southeast Asia Department
                          Urban Development and Water Division, SERD

D. Community-Driven Development Support Project

Project No.   :   46420-002 (Proposed)
Amount (US $ million) :   372
Executing Agencies   :   Department of Social Welfare and Development
Sector   :   Multisector

Status: Management Review Meeting scheduled on 18 April 2013

Impact: Reduced average poverty incidence in the poorest areas of the country

Outcome: Communities in targeted poor municipalities empowered to improve access to services and to participate in more inclusive local planning, budgeting and implementation

Outputs:
1. CDD subprojects identified and completed
2. Institutional and organizational capacity strengthened
3. Program management and M&E systems enhanced

Business Opportunities
- Consulting Services: To be determined

- Procurement: To be determined

Responsible ADB Officer: Joel V. Mangahas (E-mail: jmangahas@adb.org)
                                 Southeast Asia Department
                                 Human and Social Development Division, SERD

E. Water District Development Sector Project

Project No.   :   41665-013 (Proposed)
Amount (US $ million) :   120
Executing Agencies   :   Local Water Utilities Administration
Sector   :   Water Supply and Sanitation

Status: Management Review Meeting on 16 August 2013

Project Rationale and Linkage to Country/Regional Strategy: The Philippines is one of the few countries in Asia that is blessed with fresh water abundance. Although the amount of raw water available is more than the demand, a significant percentage of the population does not have adequate and sustained access to potable water supply. Prevailing problems of excessive and wasteful use, pollution of sources, illegal connections and inefficiencies in the distribution are but some of the causes of the shortages. The extent of water supply coverage and population access to safe drinking water in the Philippines cannot be accurately ascertained, due to variances in estimates made by the different government offices. However, the general trend is that coverage levels have declined over the past few years, from about 81% in 2000 to 79% in 2005. Outside of Metro Manila, piped water services are provided by a total of 6,280 water service providers (WSP) including 580 water districts (WD), 1,000 LGU-run utilities, 500 Rural Waterworks and Sanitation Associations (RWSA), 3,100 Barangay Water and Sanitation Associations (BWSA), 200 Cooperatives, and 900 private firms. Presidential Decree (PD) 198 of 1973 created the Local Water Utilities Administration (LWUA) and the WD concept, for LWUA to be a specialized lending and technical advisory institutions for WDs. While WDs are generally better performing than the other forms of WSP, there is still need for investment in water supply infrastructure development, and utility performance improvement. Coverage for access to sanitation ranged from 72% to 86.2 % in 2004, depending on the source of data. Although more than half of Filipino households have septic tanks, these are often poorly constructed and not maintained properly. Less than 1% of septic tanks are known to undergo regular de-sludging and the appropriate treatment. Outside of Metro Manila, only three cities (Baguio, Vigan and Zamboanga) have sewer systems, and serving less than 3% of their service area population. The current situation is that domestic wastewater largely goes untreated and that the majority of the population is exposed to raw sewage. Most water utilities focus only on water supply services. While LGUs are mandated to provide essential services, including water and sanitation services, 97% of their investments are for water supply and only 3% for sanitation and wastewater treatment.

Impact: Improved public health

Outcome: Increased access to water supply and sanitation services in the communities served by participating WDs.

Outputs:
- Extension and improvement of the water supply system
- Increased awareness about sanitation, and pilot sanitation projects
- Capacity and institutional development for participating WDs and LWUA

Business Opportunities
- Consulting Services: To be determined

- Procurement: To be determined

Responsible ADB Officer: Stella Tansengco-Schapero (E-mail: sschapero@adb.org)
Southeast Asia Department
Urban Development and Water Division, SERD

SRI LANKA

Education Sector Development Program

Loan No.	:	**3008, 3009**
Project No.	:	**39293-037**
Amount (US $ million)	:	**200**
Executing Agencies	:	**Ministry of Education**
Sector	:	**Multisector**

Status: Board approved on 27 June 2013

Description: The proposed results-based lending (RBL) program will support the Government of Sri Lanka in equitably developing its human capital base in order to meet the objectives of the Mahinda Chintana: Vision for the Future and the National Human Resources and Employment Policy (NHREP) for Sri Lanka. The proposed program will support the government's Education Sector Development Framework and Program (ESDFP), which seeks to transform the school education system to create a human capital foundation for a knowledge economy. It builds on the extensive experience of the Asian Development Bank (ADB) in Sri Lanka's education sector.

Project Rationale and Linkage to Country/Regional Strategy: The RBL program is highly relevant and justified as it: (i) builds on past investment experience to support fundamental, second-generation reforms in education quality; (ii) is aligned with the country programming strategy, 2012-2016; (iii) provides sector-wide predictable and sustainable financing for the ESDFP expenditure framework, which has strong government ownership; (iv) enhances the leverage of the education sector to secure adequate and predictable financing from the Ministry of Finance and Planning (MOFP); and (v) supports institutional development of the sector by incrementally strengthening program implementation and fiduciary systems to improve efficiency and manage risks adequately.

Impact: Enhanced youth employability in Sri Lanka

Outcome: A modernized secondary education school system developed

Outputs:
- Improved student learning;
- Improved equity and efficiency of the school system;
- Strengthened school leadership;
- Strengthened capacity for effective program planning and implementation

Responsible ADB Officer: Sofia Shakil (E-mail: sshakil@adb.org)
South Asia Department
Human and Social Development Division, SARD

TURKMENISTAN

Zerger Regional Power Generation Project

Project No.	:	**44184-013 (Proposed)**
Amount (US $ million)	:	**150**
Executing Agencies	:	**Turkmenenergo**
Sector	:	**Energy**

Status: Proposed; management review meeting scheduled on October 2, 2012

Description: The Regional Power Interconnection Project will address electric supply needs in Afghanistan (AFG) and electric infrastructure development and export plans in Turkmenistan (TKM). The Project will meet AFG needs as: (i) development partners have advised plans for investment in transmission and distribution which will increase the low electrification rate thereby increasing demand (ii) development of new domestic generation is not expected to meet forecast demand, (iii) existing interconnections cannot fill the supply gap, and (iv) electric imports from TKM can meet new demand in a cost effective manner while increasing security by diversifying import sources. The Project will allow TKM utilize its gas reserves for electric exports by adding additional gas fired generating plant. The Project will increase generation capacity in TKM and interconnect the electric grid systems of TKM and the AFG thereby allowing TKM to export electric energy to AFG. In TKM, the Project includes a new gas-fired 300MW combined cycle power plant. In AFG, the project includes new transmission lines and substations in its western region including a connection from the TKM/AFG border to the existing 220kV grid. The specific components of the Project will be confirmed by a Project Preparatory Technical Assistance (PPTA).

Impact: Increased regional cooperation and optimized use of regional energy resources

Outcome: In TKM, increased generation efficiency and improved access to export markets. In AFG, enhanced security of supply and supply reliability

Outputs: Power Purchase Sales Agreement (PPSA) New Serdar power plant in TKM located at Zergar or Atamyrat New 500-kV line in AFG from TKM/AFG border to Naidabad

Business Opportunities

- Consulting Services: All consultants will be engaged following the Guidelines on the Use of Consultants by Asian Development Bank and its Borrowers (2010, as amended from time to time). Consulting firms will be recruited using quality- and cost-based selection, with a quality-cost ratio of 90:10 required due to the complex nature of the consulting tasks and with the project having critical downstream impact.

- Procurement: All goods and works will be procured by international competitive bidding. The turnkey power plant package ($400 million) will be jointly financed by IDB. It is expected that IDB will finance the gas turbines, heat recovery system generators, and steam turbine components of the power plant while ADB will finance the remaining components. To enable such joint procurement, it is proposed to expand country eligibility for procurement by allowing firms, subcontractors, and sourcing of materials from any country eligible under ADB's Procurement Guidelines (2010, as amended from time to time) and IDB's Guidelines for Procurement of Goods and Works under IDB Financing (2009). This requires a waiver under Article 14 (ix) of the Agreement Establishing the Asian Development Bank.

Responsible ADB Officer: Jim Liston (E-mail: jliston@adb.org)
Central and West Asia Department
Energy Division, CWRD

UZBEKISTAN

Takhiatash Power Plant Efficiency Improvement Project

Project No.	:	**45306-001 (Proposed)**
Amount (US $ million)	:	**200**
Executing Agencies	:	**UzbekEnergo**
Sector	:	**Multisector**

Status: Proposed; management review meeting scheduled on August 15, 2013

Description: The objective of the proposed project is to improve energy efficiency of the Takhiatash thermal power plant (TPP) with the adoption of energy efficient technology that will contribute to increased reliable power supply and climate change mitigation. The project will include construction of a combined cycle gas turbine (CCGT) power plant, decommissioning of inefficient existing power plant units, and capacity development.

Project Rationale and Linkage to Country/Regional Strategy: Uzbekistan's power generation plants are generally old and inefficient, requiring urgent modernization. More than 75% of the power plant units are over 30 years old reaching or exceeding their economic life. The thermal efficiency averages 31%, while that of energy efficient CCGT exceeds 50%. Replacing the existing power generation assets with energy efficient equipment is a key strategy for saving energy, securing reliable power supply, and reducing greenhouse gas (GHG) emission. To this end, State Joint-Stock Company Uzbekenergo (Uzbekenergo), a 100% government-owned vertically integrated utility company, has developed a $5.3 billion investment plan (2011-2015) that includes construction of 15 thermal power plants (2,412 megawatt [MW]). The project that constructs a 280 MW CCGT is a priority project identified under this investment plan. The 730 MW TPP is the main power supply source for the Karakalpakstan and Khorezm regions with over 3 million people located in the western part of Uzbekistan. The power demand outlook is strong with a number of industrial development projects envisaged for the region, exceeding currently available capacity. In the medium term, the transmission capacity for the region also needs to be expanded, and power generation capacity of Takhiatash TPP needs to be further expanded. Out of the gas-fired five steam turbine units in operation at Takhiatash TPP, three units built in 1969 (two units of 100 MW) and 1974 (one unit of 110 MW) are some of the oldest units in operation with 23.7% efficiency. After the new power unit becomes operational, these units will be decommissioned. Decommissioning requires careful planning and implementation without disrupting reliable power supply and in compliance with safety and environmental standards, as well as cost effectiveness consideration. Uzbekenergo is improving its organizational performance through the assistance of ADB. The investment unit will be restructured. Financial transparency will be improved through introducing financial reporting and auditing that complies with international standards. Further restructuring envisages a more efficient cost-centered approach. Management and planning systems will be modernized to increase its operational performance. The electricity tariffs have been raised continuously since 2004 to ensure full cost recovery. The introduction of advanced electricity metering will further strengthen financial sustainability. Notwithstanding, further reform efforts are necessary. Uzbekenergo faces a $1.6 billion funding gap to fulfill its $5.3 billion investment plan. It needs to develop a strategy and build the capacity to attract and raise investment funds required to transform its infrastructure facilities into efficient assets. While there is a substantial opportunity, knowledge and technical capacity to attract investment funding, including climate change funds and carbon financing, are limited. The project follows the ADB's strategy for Uzbekistan, which includes focus on energy efficiency and reliable power supply. It is also consistent with ADB's Strategy 2020 and ADB Energy Policy (2009) by promoting energy efficiency and energy for all. It will be ADB's fourth project loan intervention in Uzbekistan's power sector.

Impact: Improved reliable power supply

Outcome: Increased energy efficient power supply in Karakalpakstan and Khorezm regions

Outputs:
1. Operational energy efficient power unit in Takhiatash TPP
2. Enhanced Uzbekenergo s investment funding capacity

Business Opportunities
- Consulting Services: A supervision consulting firm will be recruited using the quality- and cost-based selection method, with a 90:10 ratio for quality and cost, and following ADB's Guidelines on the Use of Consultants (2010, as amended from time to time) to help the executing agency implement the project.

- Procurement: A turnkey contractor, which is expected to undertake both the construction and decommissioning works, will be selected under international competitive bidding, following ADB's Procurement Guidelines (2010, as amended from time to time).

Responsible ADB Officer: Keiju Mitsuhashi (E-mail: kmitsuhashi@adb.org)
Central and West Asia Department
Energy Division, CWRD

III. TECHNICAL ASSISTANCE

PLEASE NOTE: Please click on the project title to access full project information. Technical assistance (TA) is used to prepare and implement projects, and support advisory and regional activities of the bank. ADB is no longer issuing TA project alerts classified according to type, i.e., project preparatory technical assistance (PPTA), advisory technical assistance (ADTA), etc. If you want to know the specific TA classification, please contact our office or inquire directly with the bank.

AFGHANISTAN

Gas Development Master Plan

TA No.	:	8401
Project No.	:	47018-001
Amount (US $ million)	:	0.8
Executing Agencies	:	Ministry of Mines Wahidullah Shahrani, Minister
Sector	:	Energy

Status: Board approved on 11 July 2013

Description: There is a critical need to develop a gas sector master plan for Afghanistan's emerging gas sector. The master plan would cover a 20-year horizon (2015-2035) and would entail: (i) preparation of gas demand and supply outlook and scenarios; (ii) development of market assessments and netback analysis; (iii) review current policies and plans in context of gas development; (iv) assessment of the financial requirements and needs; (v) evaluation of pricing options for various segments viz domestic sales and transit/exports; (vi) develop a planning model and train Ministry of Mines and Petroleum staff on its use; (vii) assessment of environmental, socioeconomic, and non-monetary impacts; (viii) review of other countries' experiences with gas supply chain development including compressed natural gas (CNG) sector; and (ix) formulation of an Afghanistan Gas Sector Master Plan and Implementation Strategy (with sequencing of priority investment projects).

Impact: Improved energy security in Afghanistan

Outcome: Improved Ministry of Mines and Petroleum capacity in the areas of investment planning and programming in gas sector supply chain

Outputs: A gas development master plan with the following features:
- Assessment of gas resource potential (indigenous and possible importation options) and its optimized economic use and environmental impact;
- Determination of major allocation sectors and load centers, including gas demand forecast for a 20-year period (2015-2035);
- Formulation of strategy for upstream, midstream and downstream gas sector development;
- Identification of investment projects to sustain Afghan gas sector and its linkages with power sector investments;
- Preparation of capacity development plan for Ministry of Mines and Petroleum to sustain gas sector master planning in Afghanistan

Business Opportunities
- Consulting Services: Recruitment of the consultant firm will be undertaken using quality-based selection by full technical proposal in accordance with ADB's Guidelines on the Use of Consultants (April 2010, as amended from time to time).

- Procurement: To be determined

Responsible ADB Officer: Asad Aleem (E-mail: aaleem@adb.org)
Central and West Asia Department
Energy Division, CWRD

BANGLADESH

Regional Power Generation and Transmission Project (formerly Energy Efficiency Improvement II)

Project No.	:	41160-012 (Proposed)
Amount (US $ million)	:	1.5
Sector	:	Energy

Project details to be determined.

Status: Not provided by ADB

Responsible ADB Officer: Hongwei Zhang (E-mail: hwzhang@adb.org)
South Asia Department
Energy Division, SARD

CHINA

A. Shanxi Technical and Vocational Education and Training Development Project

TA No.	:	8399
Project No.	:	47029-001
Amount (US $ million)	:	0.75
Executing Agencies	:	Shanxi Provincial Government
Sector	:	Education

Status: Board approved on 4 July 2013

Description: Located in the central region of the People s Republic of China (PRC), Shanxi is a less developed province with a population of 36 million. In 2011, Shanxi's gross domestic product per capita ranked 18th in the PRC and 18.8% of Shanxi s rural dwellers lived below the national poverty line, significantly higher than the national average of 13.4%. As one of the PRC's key energy and industrial bases, Shanxi has contributed to the energy supply and industrial development in the PRC. The province s key industries include coal, metallurgy, coal-fired power generation, and machinery. However, Shanxi's resource-based economy is characterized by low-technology manufacturing, high energy consumption, and a significant contribution to environmental degradation. In 2010, the PRC State Council designated Shanxi as a national pilot reform zone for the transformation of a resource-based economy. This provides a significant opportunity to foster innovation and industrial upgrading, expand and modernize the services and agricultural sectors, and support an inclusive and environmentally sustainable growth. To achieve these objectives, Shanxi needs a multi-skilled workforce. Strengthening human resources through the development of technical and vocational education and training (TVET) is one of the key priorities under the PRC 's and Shanxi' s 12th Five-Year Plans, 2011- 2015. Currently, Shanxi is facing a severe shortage of highly skilled workers in priority sectors and emerging areas. Under the provincial 12th Five-Year Plan, Shanxi is expected to further reduce the number of coal mining sites and to automate extraction in 70% of the coal mines. This planned technological upgrading and the need to ensure coal mining safety has resulted in a shortage of 200,000 highly skilled workers in the coal industry. In manufacturing, the provincial development plans emphasize renewable energy, biotechnology, new materials, and advanced equipment manufacturing, which are in line with national level strategic industries. To move up the value chain and diversify the production structure, it is essential to improve research and development capacity and to train high and medium skilled workers. Given Shanxi's central geographic location, the province plans to accelerate development of the rail and air freight transport systems, multimodal transport hubs, and distribution and logistics centers to achieve an interconnected network. There is a demand for more skilled workers to further improve its logistics system. Further, with abundant cultural and natural heritage sites, Shanxi is well positioned to develop a modern tourism industry; however, a lack of skilled workers has been a constraint to further development of tourism. There is a need to retrain migrants and displaced workers from small coal mines to improve livelihoods.

Business Opportunities
- Consulting Services: In accordance with the two-phase approach described above, the consulting services provided under the TA will be grouped into two for phase one and phase two respectively. Phase one will provide 5.0 person-months of international and 7.0 person-months of national consulting services to conduct a review of the TVET sector in Shanxi for the project. The consulting services under phase one will be engaged by ADB on an individual consultant basis, in accordance with ADB Guidelines on the Use of Consultants (2010, as amended from time to time), to ensure immediate mobilization to facilitate project scoping. For phase two, an international consulting firm will be engaged in accordance with ADB s Guidelines on the Use of Consultants. ADB will select and engage the consultants based on the quality of the proposal (90%) and the cost (10%) of the services to be provided (the quality- and cost-based selection method) using the simplified technical proposal procedure. The 90:10 weighting is considered appropriate because it is expected that the proposed project will have a strong impact on the development of the TVET system in Shanxi and can serve as a model for replication in other provinces and autonomous regions of the PRC, and therefore requires high-quality technical inputs. A total of 34.5 person-months of consulting services (13.0 international and 21.5 national) will be recruited as Phase II consultants. The consultants will provide expertise in TVET, labor market analysis, CBC, industry-school collaboration, training of instructors, management of TVET, finance and economics, poverty and social assessment and development, resettlement, environment, institutional development, construction engineering, and project management.

- Procurement: To be determined

Responsible ADB Officer: Antonio Ressano Garcia (E-mail: aressano@adb.org)
East Asia Department
Urban and Social Sectors Division, EARD

B. Strengthening Capacity for Low-Carbon Development in Ningbo

TA No.   :   8388
Project No.   :   47055-001
Amount (US $ million) :   0. 5
Executing Agencies   :   **Ningbo Municipal Government**
                               Wu Bohua, Deputy Division Chief

Sector   :   **Education**

Status: Board approved on 21 June 2013

Description: The capacity development technical assistance (CDTA) will address the critical capacity gaps of NMG in designing and implementing a low-carbon development strategy through targeted package of policy, regulations, and financial incentives in promoting industrial energy efficiency and accelerate distributed renewable energy generation. The CDTA will also enhance NMG s capacity in structuring PPPs for clean energy investments through appropriate allocation of responsibilities and risks between private and public sector entities. The CDTA will identify technologies and industrial processes to achieve the benchmark energy efficiency levels and assist NMG in establishing a technology transfer mechanism through technology providers, such as energy service companies (ESCOs). Since the ESCOs have the right technical expertise on appropriate technologies but are constrained by access to debt financing, the CDTA will be developing innovative financial products and instruments and recommend the establishment of a dedicated financing platform to mobilize financing for energy efficiency projects implemented by ESCOs and SMEs overcoming prevailing barriers. If successful, it can be introduced and replicated in other parts of the PRC. Integration of distributed renewable energy sources poses a number of technical, institutional, and financial challenges for investments to flow in scattered but large number of small-scale renewable energy projects compared to a single large-scale project. The role of private investments in such projects cannot be emphasized enough. The proposed CDTA will review the current policy framework to introduce appropriate policy incentives through transparent regulatory regime, feed-in tariffs, and tax incentives to promote private sector investments through PPPs in distributed renewable energy.

Business Opportunities
- Consulting Services: The technical assistance (TA) will be implemented in two phases. Phase 1 will help the NMG identify strategies, initiatives, and financial products that need to be launched as early actions under the LCDAP. Phase 2 will support: (i) policy formulation and the design of institutional arrangements to deliver the financial products identified under phase 1, and (ii) the preparation of PPP transactions in clean energy and capacity strengthening in government agencies, financial institutions, and potential investors toward encouraging private investments in clean energy. Due to the urgency of finalizing the Ningbo LCDAP, Phase 1 will be implemented by a team of individual consultants to be recruited by ADB and consisting of two international consultants contracted for a total of 6 person-months and four national consultants, also contracted for 6 person-months. For phase 2, ADB will engage a consulting firm to supply two international consultants for a total of 5 person-months and five national consultants for 13 person-months. The TA will be implemented over 18 months, with phase 1 undertaken from 1 July to 31 December 2013 and phase 2 from 1 January to 31 December 2014. The consultants recruited for phases 1 and 2 will have extensive knowledge and expertise regarding: (i) energy efficiency project preparation and due diligence, (ii) distributed renewable energy technologies and implementation models for distributed renewable energy projects, (iii) how to structure PPP projects for renewable energy and energy efficiency investments, (iv) financial regulations governing SME financing in the PRC, and (v) structuring financial products to overcome the barriers faced by ESCOs. The consulting firm for phase 2 will be engaged using quality- and

cost-based selection with a quality cost ratio of 90:10, as the experience and expertise of the consultants in designing innovative financial products is highly relevant to achieving TA objectives. Selection will be based on a simplified technical proposal. Consultant recruitment will accord with ADB Guidelines on the Use of Consultants (2010, as amended from time to time). TA funds will be disbursed in line with the Technical Assistance Disbursement Handbook (2010, as amended from time to time).

- Procurement: To be determined

Responsible ADB Officer: Pradeep Perera (E-mail: pperera@adb.org)
East Asia Department
Energy Division, EARD

MYANMAR

Design of e-Governance Master Plan and Review of Information and Communication Technology Capacity in Academic Institutions

TA No.	:	8398
Project No.	:	47158-001
Amount (US $ million)	:	0.5
Executing Agencies	:	Ministry of Science and Technology Ministry of Communications &Information Technology
Sector	:	Multisector

Status: Board approved on 4 July 2013

Impact: Enhanced service delivery capacity and efficient public management of the public services in the country

Outcome: Adoption of an integrated approach in implementing government applications and online services to achieve enhanced capacity for public service delivery

Outputs:
- Design of e-Governance Master plan and action items
- Develop sustainability action plan for ICT capacity enhancements in the identified ICT academic institutions
- Develop at least one demonstration initiative and knowledge transfer in one ICT academic institution

Business Opportunities
- Procurement: To be determined

- Consulting Services: To be determined

Responsible ADB Officer: Arun Ramamurthy (E-mail: rarun@adb.org)
Regional and Sustainable Development Department
Public Management, Governance and Participation Div., RSDD

PAKISTAN

Jalalpur Irrigation Project

TA No.	:	8404
Project No.	:	46528-001
Amount (US $ million)	:	0.8
Executing Agencies	:	Irrigation and Power Dept., Punjab
		Mr. Khalid Masood, Secretary

Sector : **Agriculture and Natural Resources**

Status: Board approved on 18 July 2013

Description: The government carried out a preliminary feasibility study in 2008, which lacks in appropriate assessment of social and environmental safeguards, biodiversity, groundwater, drainage, institutional development, on-farm water and agriculture and climate change related issues.

<u>Business Opportunities</u>
- Procurement: To be determined

- Consulting Services: The consulting service shall be provided through (a) consultancy firm mainly for feasibility study and (b) IO/NGO for institutional, on-farm and capacity building components. The PPTA will provide 80 person-months through consultancy firm(s) and 14 person-months of IO/NGO. The consultants will be recruited in accordance with ADB's Guidelines on the Use of Consultants (2010, as amended from time to time). The consultancy firm will be selected through quality- and cost-based selection (QCBS) method (90:10). A simplified technical proposal will be requested from the shortlisted firms. The IO will be recruited through quality-based selection (QBS) as (i) on-farm and institutional component will have overriding influence on the outcome of the project, (ii) not many suitably experienced IOs available in Pakistan and (iii) proposed assignment can be carried out in different ways, which may constrain comparison of financial proposal. The selected IO will recruit a national non-governmental organization (NGO) for social mobilization and community communication and coordination. A provisional sum will be allocated in the contract of IO for the recruitment of the NGO. ADB fact-finding mission in March 2013 identified two potential relevant international organizations i.e. International Center for Agricultural Research in the Dry Area (ICARDA) and International Water Management Institute (IWMI) and one NGO i.e. National Rural Support Program (NRSP) due to their experience in on-farm agricultural and water management and community mobilization, presence in the project area and knowledge of local issues and community. The mission agreed the inclusion of IO/NGO services with the Government.

Responsible ADB Officer: Akhtar Ali (E-mail: aali@adb.org)
Central and West Asia Department
Environment, Natural Resources & Agriculture Division, CWRD

PHILIPPINES

A. Supporting Capacity Development for the Bureau of Internal Revenue (BIR)

TA No.	:	8354
Project No.	:	46429-001
Amount (US $ million) :		1
Executing Agencies	:	Philippine Country Office
Sector	:	Public sector management

Status: Board approved on 12 April 2013

Impact: Increase tax revenues

Outcome: BIR has improved capacity to mobilize tax revenues

Outputs:
  ▪ International best practices on staff training and tax administration shared
  ▪ A training strategy and medium-term training plan
  ▪ Revised training materials
  ▪ Training for trainers' seminar
  ▪ A new training course for new recruits

Business Opportunities
  ▪ Consulting Services: A total of 26 person-months (intermittent) of international consulting services and 24 person-months (intermittent) of national consulting services will be required to ensure the effective implementation of this TA.

  ▪ Procurement: To be determined

Responsible ADB Officer: Norio Usui (E-mail: nusui@adb.org)
            Southeast Asia Department
            Philippines Country Office

B. Education Improvement Sector Development Program

Project No.	:	45089-001 (Proposed)
Amount (US $ million) :		1.5
Executing Agencies	:	Department of Education
Sector	:	Multisector

Project details to be determined by ADB

Business Opportunities
  ▪ Consulting Services: The project preparatory technical assistance (PPTA) will recruit individual consultants and a consulting firm (QCBS, 80:20) to implement the PPTA. Consultant engagement will be sequenced to ensure timely delivery of ADB support. Consultant requirements are estimated at 34.5 person-months of international consultant inputs and 50.5 person-months of national consultant inputs. Consultant recruitment will be phased. Some international and national consultants will be engaged as individual consultants and will be recruited by January 2012: (i) the Secondary Education Policy, System Reform and Finance

specialists; (ii) the Education Facilities and Infrastructure PPP specialists; and (iii) the Education Service Delivery PPP specialists.

- Procurement Notices: To be determined

Responsible ADB Officer: Norman LaRocque (E-mail: nlarocque@adb.org)
Southeast Asia Department
Human and Social Development Division, SERD

C. PFM 3 [previously Governance and Public Financial Management Phase I (Cluster TA)]

Project No.	:	43398-012 (Proposed)
Executing Agencies	:	Department of Education
Sector	:	Multisector

Status: Fact-finding scheduled on 28 Jun 2011 to 29 Jun 2011

Details to be determined

Business Opportunities:
- Consulting services: To be determined

- Procurement: To be determined

Responsible ADB Officer: Kelly Bird (E-mail: kbird@adb.org)
Southeast Asia Department
Public Management, Financial Sector and Trade Division, SERD

D. The Procter & Gamble Company Waste to Worth Project

Loan No.	:	8117
Project No.	:	46927-012
Executing Agencies	:	The Procter & Gamble Company
Sector	:	Multisector

Status: Board approved on 17 July 2012

Description: The project preparatory technical assistance (PPTA) will partly finance site-specific feasibility studies for two waste-to-energy projects located in Angeles City, Pamapanga and Antipolo City, Rizal.

Project Rationale and Linkage to Country/Regional Strategy: One objective of ADB s country partnership strategy for the Philippines which is to reduce environmental degradation and vulnerability to climate change and disasters. To achieve this, ADB will support investment needs to ensure sustainable financing of infrastructure and foster development of sustainable communities; ADB assistance aims to strengthen waste management and flood control systems among others. PSOD, in particular, is in search of commercially viable solutions and partners who have the financial capacity and are willing to experiment and innovate in this area. The proposed PPTA is consistent with this objective improving sustainable environmental infrastructure in highly urbanized areas where economic gains can be maximized. It will also incentivize private sector participation in addressing MSW problem.

Outputs: The output of the PPTA is satisfactory completion of the feasibility study, supporting the development of the two WTE project in Antipolo City and Angeles City.

Business Opportunities:
- Consulting services: To be determined

- Procurement: To be determined

Responsible ADB Officer: Jose Manuel Limjap (E-mail: jmlimjap@adb.org)
Private Sector Operations Department
Infrastructure Finance Division 2

E. Climate Resilience and Green Growth in Critical Watersheds

Project No.	:	**46441-001 (Proposed)**
Amount (US $ million)	:	**1.73**
Executing Agencies	:	**Asian Development Bank**
Sector	:	**Multisector**

Status: Concept Clearance scheduled on 1 March 2013

Description: The proposed technical assistance (TA) is aimed at strengthening the capacity of LGUs in critical watersheds including the lower Marikina river basin, Camarines Sur and Davao Oriental. These areas are chosen based on their: (i) high bio-physical vulnerability to climate change impacts; (ii) high levels of urban poverty and population density with settlements in vulnerable locations; and (iii) high demonstration potential to the rest of the country, in terms of mainstreaming climate resilience and green growth in local development at policy and operational levels. The proposed TA includes stocktaking and vision setting in creation of a green growth road map for each.

Project Rationale and Linkage to Country/Regional Strategy: The TA supports the Philippines National Climate Change Action Plan (NCCAP) for 2011-2028, which anchors on building ecologically stable and economically resilient towns. The TA supports the implementation of the Philippines Climate Change Act (Republic Act No. 9729), which aims at mainstreaming climate risk reduction into national, sector and local development plans and programs. The TA has strong links to the Philippines development plan, 2011-2016, especially with regard to goal 3 (enhanced resilience of natural systems and improved adaptive capacities of human communities to cope with environmental hazards, including climate-related risks) of the strategic framework for conservation, protection, and rehabilitation of the environment and natural resources.

Impact: Enhanced climate resilience and green growth in critical watersheds

Outcome: Improved ability of LGUs and other stakeholders to mainstream climate resilient and green growth options into development programs, plans and policies

Outputs:
- GHG inventory and assessment of vulnerabilities to climate change at LGU level
- Gender-responsive priority measures for adaptation and GHG mitigation for each LGU Selection of pilot areas and demonstration of priority climate change actions
- Climate change knowledge products to enhance technical capacity

Business Opportunities:
- Consulting Services: The technical assistance (TA) will be implemented over 30 months from 1 October 2013 to 31 March 2016 and will require an estimated 14 person-months of international and 200 person-months of national consultant inputs, to be engaged through a consulting firm in

accordance with ADB's Guidelines on the Use of Consultants (2010, as amended from time to time).

- Procurement: Procurement and disbursement will be done in accordance with ADB s Procurement Guidelines (April 2010, as amended from time to time) and ADB's Technical Assistance Disbursement Handbook (May 2010, as amended from time to time).

Responsible ADB Officer: Ancha Srinivasan (E-mail: asrinivasan@adb.org)
Southeast Asia Department
Environment, Natural Resources & Agriculture Division, SERD

F. Second Road Improvement & Institutional Development Project

Project No.	:	**41076-045 (Proposed)**
Amount (US $ million)	:	**0.9**
Executing Agencies	:	**Asian Development Bank**
Sector	:	**Transport and ICT**

Project details to be determined by ADB

Business Opportunities:
- Consulting Services: To be determined

- Procurement Notices: To be determined

Responsible ADB Officer: Jeffrey M. Miller (E-mail: jmiller@adb.org)
Southeast Asia Department, Transport and Communications Division, SERD

G. Water District Development Sector Project

Loan No.	:	**7122**
Project No.	:	**41665-012**
Amount (US $ million)	:	**1.2**
Executing Agencies	:	**Local Water Utilities Administration**
Sector	:	**Water Supply and Sanitation**

Status: Board approved on 10 September 2008

Description: The project preparatory technical assistance (PPTA) will prepare a loan project suitable for ADB to consider financing. The ensuing loan will help improve living conditions of the urban population outside Metro Manila, enhance competitiveness by developing water supply infrastructure, and provide capacity building of water utilities. It will also support the reorganization and institutional development of LWUA, and contribute to sector reform.

Project Rationale and Linkage to Country/Regional Strategy: The proposed Water District Development Project (WDDP): (i) will continue ADB's long-term cooperation with LWUA; (ii) is in line with the CSP (2005-2007) and ADB's Water Financing Program; (iii) is in line with the Government's objective to provide improved water supply to the country (Medium-Term Philippine Development Plan 2004-2010); and (iv) will support achievement of related targets of the Millennium Development Goals (MDG).

Impact: Improved livability and competitiveness in urban areas outside Metro Manila due to better water supply and sanitation infrastructure and the sustainable provision of safe water supply and sanitation services.

Outcome: Design of the ensuing loan project agreed upon by LWUA, the Government, and the Asian Development Bank.

Business Opportunities:
- Consulting Services: The PPTA will require 92 person-months of consulting services, including 22 international and 70 national consultants. ADB will engage the consultants through a firm.

- Procurement Notices: To be determined

Responsible ADB Officer: Rudolf Frauendorfer (E-mail: rfrauendorfer@adb.org)
Southeast Asia Department
Urban Development and Water Division, SERD

H. Support for Data Management for Performance Reporting and Assessment

TA No.	:	8397
Project No.	:	47193-001
Amount (US $ million)	:	0.23
Executing Agencies	:	**Department of Budget and Management**
Sector	:	**Public sector management**

Status: Board approved on 4 July 2013

Description: The small-scale technical assistance (S-TA) is designed to support the Department of Budget and Management to move forward with its information technology initiatives and to drive performance-based management initiatives in national government agencies through the development of an accessible data base.

Impact: National government expenditures are results-based

Outcome: A performance indicator registry is institutionalized in the Department of Budget and Management

Outputs:
- Performance Indicator Register fields completed
- Draft data management manual and recommend organizational unit responsibility available
- Concept paper on use of Major Final Output
- Performance Indicators in the Performance-Based Bonus available to Department of Budget and Management

Business Opportunities
Procurement: To be determined

Consulting Services: (i) Results-Based Management (RBM) Specialist (International, 4PM, intermittent, August 2013-May 2014); (ii) Results-Based Budgeting Specialist (National, 3PM, intermittent, August 2013-May 2014); (iii) Results-Based Budgeting Specialist (National, 3PM, intermittent, August 2013-May 2014); (iv) Performance-Based Remuneration Specialist (International, 1PM, intermittent, August 2013-May 2014)

Responsible ADB Officer: Claudia Buentjen (E-mail: cbuentjen@adb.org)
Southeast Asia Department
Philippines Country Office

REGIONAL

A. Provision of Knowledge Products and Services to DMCs through Systematic Knowledge Sharing

TA No.	:	8392
Project No.	:	46244-001
Amount (US $ million)	:	0.5
Executing Agencies	:	Asian Development Bank
Sector	:	Multisector

Status: Board approved on 30 May 2013

Description: Knowledge plays a vital role in driving economic growth and achieving development outcomes. Provision of knowledge products and services (KPS) has been a key part of ADB's development assistance. In 2008, ADB made knowledge solutions one of the drivers of change in Strategy 2020. Subsequently, ADB undertook a number of initiatives to scale up and strengthen its knowledge operations. One of these initiatives is the establishment of the Knowledge Sharing and Services Center (KSSC). Part of KSSC s mandate is to deliver knowledge sharing and support services in ADB and for DMCs by enhancing internal knowledge sharing and developing external knowledge sharing and partnerships.

Project Rationale and Linkage to Country/Regional Strategy: This technical assistance is proposed to support provision of KPS to DMCs through systematic knowledge sharing.

Impact: Greater development effectiveness of ADB operations and of development projects of DMCs and more informed development policy-making in DMCs.

Outcome: Increased capacity in ADB to capture and apply knowledge embedded in its operations and more knowledge sharing among think tanks in developing Asia.

Outputs:
- Capturing ADB's Operations Knowledge: Proposal of a model to extract embedded knowledge in ADB operations
- Capturing ADB's Operations Knowledge: Launch of demonstrative knowledge products
- Asia Think Tanks Networking: Establishment of a network of Asian think tanks for sharing knowledge, particular attention will be given to the needs of the low-income DMCs
- Asia Think Tanks Networking: Knowledge sharing events Asia Think Tanks Networking: Knowledge products

Business Opportunities
- Consulting Services: Consultants will be recruited, either individually or through firms. The implementation of TA activities will require the services of international consultants (up to 7 person-months, intermittent) and national consultants (up to 31 person-months, intermittent).

- Procurement: To be determined

Responsible ADB Officer: Dongxiang Li
Regional and Sustainable Development Department
RSDD-KS

B. Greater Mekong Subregion Phnom Penh Plan for Development Management Phase V

Project No.	:	46232-001
Amount (US $ million)	:	0.75
Executing Agencies	:	Asian Development Bank
Sector	:	Public sector management

Status: Board approved on January 22, 2013

Description: The Phnom Penh Plan for Development Management (PPP) is a capacity development program that supports knowledge products and services in the Greater Mekong Subregion (GMS). It is a pioneering program to build capacities of civil servants and to promote regional cooperation in the GMS. PPP has received total funding of $10.95 million since its inception in 2003 for the first four phases. It is designed as a continuing project, with each phase building on the experiences and lessons of previous phases. The PPP has had notable achievements. Learning programs provide GMS policy makers and managers with conceptual tools and frameworks on regional integration and leadership, core development sectors, development management and cross-cutting themes. These programs enhance their skills in developing and implementing functional and strategic development interventions. To date, 2,032 GMS civil servants have attended 103 PPP learning programs organized with 28 capacity development partners (within and outside the GMS). The PPP supports fellowships to prestigious universities and institutes. Graduates of these learning programs or the 47 fellows now constitute the core of development leaders who are making a difference in the GMS. Seven issues of the Journal of Greater Mekong Subregion Development Studies, a multidisciplinary peer-reviewed publication promotes better understanding of GMS development issues have been published. The PPP Research Program has funded 4 multi-country research projects (female labor quality; contract farming; financial services in border areas; and cross-border economic zones) participated by 14 GMS institutions and produced 4 working papers, 4 policy briefs and a journal special issue. The PPP organized 7 GMS Development Dialogues (GDDs) attended by 500 participants from government, civil society, academe, private sector and media to provide a platform for in-depth discussion of subregional issues to enhance policy and decision making capacities. The PPP also supports learning resource centers in Cambodia and Lao PDR with about 10,000 users and organized 18 Leaders Networking for Knowledge (LINK) alumni events with 850 participants. A program management and performance monitoring and evaluation system set up to be more results oriented. A newsletter (Mekong Leaders) published and website established. The TA builds on past experiences and lessons learned from previous phases. Several evaluation were conducted on the PPP including an evaluation study conducted by OED in 2008, the PPP Impact Assessment Study also in 2008 and TA completion reports for the first three phases. The major lessons learned include the need for: (i) selecting learning programs with more sharpened focus and customization that contribute to developing individual civil servants capacities to support GMS cooperation; (ii) better targeting of participants involved in GMS working groups, programs and projects; (iii) follow-up and deepening programs, i.e. one-off programs unlikely to lead to sustainable workplace behavior; (iv) progressively develop technical and financial sustainability; (v) more active roles of GMS institutions (both research and training), despite their weak capacities, for PPP to phase out and eventually assume a more facilitative and enabling role; (vi) developing a pool of GMS trainers and experts; (vii) GMS learning materials (e.g. case studies, manuals and tool kits); (viii) better synergies and linkages of policy research with learning programs; and (ix) better indicators (baseline and targets) for more results-oriented capacity development. These lessons were taken into account, thus the regional capacity development technical assistance (R-CDTA) design include new key features: (i) customized regional cooperation learning programs; (ii) better targeting of participants; (iii) sustainability strategies such as Training of Trainers (TOT), learning materials development and new partnership modalities; (iv) South-south cooperation focusing on low income countries; and (v) tracer studies and comprehensive evaluation.

Impact: GMS Governments design and implement effective and efficient strategies and projects to promote subregional cooperation

Outcome: GMS civil servants apply knowledge acquired and skills sets developed in their work place Implementation Progress

Outputs:
1. GMS government officials acquire knowledge and develop skills set
2. High quality research on priority GMS development issues accessible to GMS civil servants
3. Knowledge acquisition, dissemination and networking on GMS cooperation improved
4. Improved capacities of GMS institutions for sustainability
5. An effective project management and performance monitoring system

Business Opportunities
- Consulting Services: 3 national consultants (individual) for total of 54 person-months of input and 1 international consultant (individual) for 8 person-months of input

- Procurement: To be determined

Responsible ADB Officer: Alfredo Perdiguero (E-mail: aperdiguero@adb.org)
Southeast Asia Department
Thailand Resident Mission

C. Midterm Review of the Republic of Korea e-Asia and Knowledge Partnership Fund

TA No.	:	8396
Project No.	:	47170-001
Amount (US $ million)	:	0.5
Executing Agencies	:	Asian Development Bank
Sector	:	Multisector

Status: Board approved on 4 July 2013

Description: The technical assistance (TA) will review the operations of the e-Asia and Knowledge Partnership Fund (The Fund) to assess its responsiveness to the evolving assistance context. Based on lessons learned during the initial six years of implementation, eligibility criteria for the Fund will be sharpened, and the Fund administration procedures will be streamlined. This will improve not only the performance of the Fund supported TAs but also the effectiveness of the Fund operations. In addition to the mid-term review of the Fund operations, the TA will explore the potential support areas through the Fund in order to maximize the development effectiveness of the Fund operations through the more systematic and demand based intervention to DMCs. Considering the increasing demands on ICT from DMCs and limited resource of the TA, the focus will be given to the e-Asia Window for this TA. Therefore, the TA will basically focus on two parts: (i) mid-term evaluation of the Fund management and operational performance, and (ii) review and identification of potential areas of intervention through the Fund. Consulting services

Business Opportunities
- Consulting services: To be determined

- Procurement Notices: To be determined

Responsible ADB Officer: Seok Yong Yoon (E-mail: syoon@adb.org)
Regional and Sustainable Development Department
Public Management, Governance and Participation Div., RSDD

SRI LANKA

Green Power Development and Energy Efficiency Improvement Investment Program

TA No.	:	8393
Project No.	:	47037-002
Amount (US $ million)	:	0.7
Executing Agencies	:	**Ministry of Power and Energy (MOPE)**
Sector	:	**Multisector**

Status: Board approved on 25 June 2013

Description: In recent years Sri Lanka has improved its energy sector and achieved a national electrification ratio of 94% (2012) compared with 29% in 1990. But a longer-term challenge is to reduce its high dependence on expensive fossil fuel energy. The energy sector struggles to: (a) meet growing demand for electricity at a low cost and acceptable reliability rates, and (b) attain long term sustainability. The share of thermal energy in the power generation mix has increased from 6% in 1995 to 54% in 2011 that creates a high energy cost base. Demand growth has been met by expensive oil-fired thermal plants. This is not the solution to the country's energy security and environment protection in the long-term. Diversification of the generation mix, especially from renewable energy sources, improved network efficiency, and supply and demand side management is the only way to correct this situation. The transmission network also needs expansion and modernization, particularly in the former conflict-affected areas in Northern and Eastern provinces. Another challenge is to improve system reliability and cut technical losses. 33 kilovolt (kV) medium voltage (MV) network is needed to expand power supply into rural areas, where many of the poor households remain unconnected or have poor quality of supplies. The new energy agenda also targets more clean energy. This is yet another means to ensure sector sustainability in the long term. Finally, the government intends to pursue financial, managerial, and institutional reforms, in line with the Sri Lanka Electricity Act, 2009. The government intends to pursue cost recovery and expects that with the introduction of low-cost coal-fired generation it will be possible to address the current high cost of power generation and achieve cost recovery from 2018. As part of its cost recovery strategy, the government increased retail electricity tariffs by 35% on average in April 2013. While the government aims to increase supply capacity and replace expensive and inefficient oil-fired power plants by constructing the coal-fired plants, the remaining supply capacity will need to come from renewable sources (and conversion of the oil-fired plants to gas-fired plants). The 20% increase in power generation from non-conventional renewable sources will be in addition to the current 45% of the conventional hydropower and will ensure that most of electricity will be generated by domestic clean energy sources in the future. This will address the critical question about the energy security agenda.

Business Opportunities
- Procurement: To be determined

- Consulting Services: A consulting firm will be recruited for the TA project with 17.5 person-months for international and 19.0 person-months for national consultants. Taking into consideration the complexity of the investment program, the firm will be recruited using quality and cost based selection methodology with a 90:10 technical-cost weighting based on simplified technical proposal. The consulting firm will conduct technical, economic, financial, and governance due diligence, prepare project cost estimates, procurement plan and implementation schedule. The international and national environmental and social development specialists will be recruited on an individual basis to ensure that that they start their field activities early in the process due to the expected environmental and involuntary resettlement categories A for the MFF. Consultants will be recruited following Guidelines on the Use of Consultants by ADB and Its Borrowers, April 2010.

Responsible ADB Officer: Mukhtor Khamudkhanov (E-mail: mkhamudkhanov@adb.org)
South Asia Department
Energy Division, SARD

VIETNAM

A. Strengthening Microfinance Sector Operations and Supervision

TA No.   :   **8391**
Project No.   :   **46482-001**
Amount (US $ million) :   **1**
Executing Agencies   :   **State Bank of Vietnam**
Sector   :   **Finance**

Status: Board Approval on 21 June 2013

Impact: Deepened financial inclusion through enhanced MFI operations

Outcome: Enhanced operational and supervisory capacity in microfinance

Outputs:
   ▪ Provided training to MFIs, CCF/PCFs, and VBSP
   ▪ Provided training to SBV, MOF and MPI supervisors
   ▪ Established a network of formal microfinance training
   ▪ Conducted knowledge sharing opportunities overseas

Business Opportunities
   ▪ Consulting Services: The technical assistance (TA) will provide 18 person-months of international consulting services and 27 person-months of national consulting services. The consultants will work on an intermittent basis and engaged in accordance with ADB's Guidelines on the Use of Consultants (2010, as amended from time to time). Disbursements under the TA will be made in accordance with ADB's Technical Assistance Disbursement Handbook (2010, as amended from time to time).

   ▪ Procurement: Equipment will be procured in accordance with ADB's Procurement Guidelines (2010, as amended from time to time).

Responsible ADB Officer: Eiichi Sasaki (E-mail: esasaki@adb.org)
Southeast Asia Department
Public Management, Financial Sector and Trade Division, SERD

B. Strengthening Support for State-Owned Enterprise Reform and Corporate Governance Facilitation Program

TA No.	:	8387
Project No.	:	39538-036
Amount (US $ million)	:	0.8
Sector	:	Public sector management

Status: Board Approval on 19 June 2013

Impact: Improved profitability of restructured SOEs and management of state managed investments.

Outcome: Improved capacity of MOF to ensure that selected SOEs are transformed into financially viable and efficiently managed enterprises.

Outputs:
1. Support MOF in conducting due diligence of selected SOEs
2. Finalizing the restructuring and implementation plans of selected SOEs
3. Developing Knowledge products for future SOE reforms in Vietnam

<u>Business Opportunities</u>
- Consulting Services: 1. International Consultants a. State-Owned Enterprise Reform and Corporate Governance Specialist Team Leader (international, 5 person-months, intermittent) b. Corporate Restructuring Specialist (international, 4.5 person-months, intermittent) c. Financial Restructuring Specialist (international, 4.5 person-months, intermittent) d. SOE Legal and Regulatory Expert (international, 2 person-months, intermittent) e. Social Safeguard Specialist (international, 2.5 person-months, intermittent)

  2. National Consultants a. SOE Reform and Corporate Restructuring Specialist (national, 12 person-months, intermittent) b. Financial Specialist (national, 12 person-months, intermittent) c. SOE Legal and Regulatory Expert (national, 6 person-months, intermittent) d. Poverty and Social Development Specialist (national, 3 person-months, intermittent) e. Gender Specialist (national, 2 person-months, intermittent) f. Social Safeguard Specialist (national, 2.5 person-months, intermittent) g. Translator and Editor (national, 5 person-months, intermittent)

- Procurement: To be determined

Responsible ADB Officer: Prasanna Kumar Jena (E-mail: pjena@adb.org)
Southeast Asia Department
Public Management, Financial Sector and Trade Division, SERD

C. Capacity Building for River Basin Water Resources Planning

Project No. : 41466-012
Amount (US $ million) : 1
Executing Agencies : **Ministry of Natural Resources and Environment**
Sector : **Multisector**

Status: Board approved on 17 January 2013

Description: The technical assistance (TA) will support the Ministry of Natural Resources and Environment's (MONRE) adoption of integrated water resources management (IWRM) principles through: (i) continued support for the revision of the LWR, and (ii) the establishment of planning tasks leading to a sector strategy and investment program for the development of the Red-Thai Binh river basin water resources. The main outputs will be the documents needed for the submission of the amended LWR by March 2011 and the planning tasks by June 2012.

Project Rationale and Linkage to Country/Regional Strategy: The TA is consistent with ADB's existing Country Partnership Strategy for Viet Nam (2007-2010), the midterm review of which called for an IWRM approach to planning strategies and work practices with ADB placing a strong focus on institutional development in conjunction with water resources infrastructure. This follows from the support provided under TA4903-VIE: Water Sector Review, which identified key water management issues and led to the formulation of Government's NTP, which specifies objectives in relation to eight programs and identifies the priority river basins. However, the elaboration of river basin development strategies and investment programs is the next step and will be addressed by the TA for the Red-Thai Binh River Basin. The TA will also continue the support for the revision of the LWR, which started under TA3892-VIE: Second Red River Basin Sector Project but closes with completion of the grant from the Netherlands at the end of October 2010. The continued support is needed to finalize the draft LWR and related documents for submission to the National Assembly in March 2011. The TA is consistent with the draft Assessment Strategy and Roadmap (ASR) for the Agriculture, Natural Resources and Environment (ANRE) Sector, which includes Natural Resources and Environment as one of the three major support areas in the ANRE Sector Development Forward Strategy. The TA will also add value to ADB's program for Viet Nam and has the potential to strengthen international cooperation with IDPs who are also working for the development of the country's water resources sector through institutional and operational capacity development.

Impact: Better management and development of the water resources sector

Outcome: Greater capacity of the Ministry of Natural Resources and Environment (MONRE) to support policy initiatives and implement investment projects

Outputs:
- Guidelines and regulations on establishing minimum flows in rivers prepared
- Planning tasks for the development of water resources of the Red-Thai Binh river basin formulated
- Documents for submission of the amended LWR prepared

Business Opportunities
- Consulting Services: The TA will require about 54 person-months of consulting services, consisting of 14 person-months international and 40 person-months national inputs for services over an implementation period of 20 months with an additional 3 months for TA closing. Existing consultants currently supporting the LWR will be extended through the firm contracted for this purpose by single source selection as the tasks involved represent a natural continuation of previous work carried out by the firm. The firm currently supporting the revision of the LWR is

Kellogg Brown & Root Pty Ltd of Australia. The firm's main role under the capacity development technical assistance (CDTA) is to provide the same six (6) consultants (5 nationals and 1 international) to continue work on the revision of the LWR, which commenced in early 2009 and has proceeded effectively with their support. The consultants to be employed on the formulation of sector strategy and investment program for the development of water resources in the Red-Thai Binh river basin will be recruited by individual consultant selection (ICS) and directly contracted by ADB. All consultants will be selected in accordance with ADB's Guidelines on the Use of Consultants (2010, as amended from time to time). Any procurement under the TA will be done in accordance with ADB's Procurement Guidelines (2010, as amended from time to time). All disbursements under the TA will be done in accordance with the ADB's Technical Assistance Disbursement Handbook (May 2010, as amended from time to time).

- Procurement: To be determined

Responsible ADB Officer: Dennis Ellingson (E-mail: dellingson@adb.org)
Southeast Asia Department
Environment, Natural Resources & Agriculture Division, SERD

IV. GRANT

AFGHANISTAN

Rehabilitation of Bamian-Yakawlang Road

Grant No.	:	**9097**
Project No.	:	**39467-012**
Amount (US $ million)	:	**20**
Executing Agencies	:	**Ministry of Public Works**
		Eng. Marzia Sulimankhel

Sector	:	**Transport and ICT**

Status: Board approved on 26 September 2006

Details: To help the Government to promote economic and social development and reduce poverty by rehabilitating the national highway network which will connect the central hinterland of Afghanistan to the ring road

Business Opportunities
- Consulting Services: To be determined

- Procurement: To be determined

Responsible ADB Officer: Zheng Wu (E-mail: zhengwu@adb.org)
Central and West Asia Department
Transport and Communications Division, CWRD

MYANMAR

GMS Capacity Building for HIV/AIDs Project (Strengthened National Response to HIV and AIDS in Myanmar)

Project No.	:	46490-001 (Proposed)
Amount (US $ million)	:	5.5
Executing Agencies	:	Ministry of Infrastructure
Sector	:	Health

Status: Management Review Meeting scheduled on 23 August 2013

Impact: Contributed to achieving and sustaining the MDG to have halted and begun to reverse the spread of HIV/AIDS in Myanmar

Outcome: Increased coverage and quality of services for targeted populations along and near the economic corridors

Outputs:
- Improved planning and management capacity at national, provincial, district and township levels
- Improved access to HIV and STI services among migrant and mobile populations and high-risk groups
- Strengthened community-based program for HIV risk reduction for key affected populations
- Monitoring and evaluation and project management

Business Opportunities
- Consulting Services: To be determined

- Procurement: To be determined

Responsible ADB Officer: Emiko Masaki (E-mail: emasaki@adb.org)
Southeast Asia Department
Human and Social Development Division, SERD

REGIONAL

Greater Mekong Subregion: Livelihood Support for Corridor Towns

Grant No.	:	9173
Project No.	:	46074-001
Amount (US $ million)	:	2.5
Executing Agencies	:	Ministry of Public Works and Transport
		Provincial People's Committee of Quang TriProvince
Sector	:	Multisector

Status: Board approved on 21 May 2013

Description: Poverty in the Greater Mekong Subregion (GMS) is still substantial in Cambodia, Lao People's Democratic Republic (Lao PDR), and Viet Nam, where its regional incidence ranges from 9% 34% of the population. Poverty in Cambodia is wide spread with approximately 30% of the rural population living below the poverty line. From 1992 to 2007, the overall national poverty incidence in Cambodia declined to about 36%, which is still a high value by regional comparison (i.e., Viet Nam's fell to 20% and Thailand's 12%). The distribution of poverty varies considerably in Cambodia, from less than 15% in the capital city to well over 45% in the northern and northeastern provinces and in the vicinity of Tonle Sap. In Battambang, the poverty incidence in 2009 was at 18%, slightly higher than in Phnom Penh (15%) but lower than the approximate national poverty incidence of 36%. Urban poverty also differs from rural poverty because the reference values in cost of living differ between urban and rural areas. Poverty in Lao PDR is still widespread with an estimated 34% of the population living under the poverty line and a large proportion of the population at risk of sliding back into poverty. In the Savannahket Province where Kaysone Phomvihane is situated, the reported poverty incidence is at 43%, higher than the national rate. Kaysone Phomvihane is also listed among the poorest districts in the Savannahket Province. Poverty is predominantly rural, with high concentrations in the remote and mountainous northeastern and eastern borders with Viet Nam, and, therefore, has a strong ethnic character. Viet Nam's progress towards reducing poverty has been impressive with the poverty incidence declining from 58% in 1993 to 10.6% in 2010. Urban poverty in Viet Nam fell from about 25% in 1993 to 4% in 2006. Rural poverty in the same period declined from 66% to 22%. However, while reductions in urban poverty in Ha Noi and Ho Chi Minh City tend to skew national averages, cities outside the major growth corridors, including those in the central provinces (Dak Lak, Pleiku, etc.), the Mekong Delta (Kien Giang, Soc Trang, etc.), the northern border (Cao Bang, Lao Cai, etc.), and the central coast (Hue, Quang Tri) still have relatively high urban poverty rates. In Dong Ha City, poverty incidence in 2010 is at 8%, higher than the national urban poverty incidence of 4%, and slightly lower than the overall poverty incidence of 10.6% in the same year. The proposed project is a pilot poverty-reduction project in the GMS using a market development approach intended to compliment the urban infrastructure investments under the three loan projects. Trade, traffic, tourism, and people flow are perceived to significantly increase in the East-West Economic Corridor (EWEC) and Southern Economic Corridor (SEC) because of the infrastructure investments under the three loan projects; the project aims to capitalize on these developments by helping poor informal traders enhance their locally-produced products and provide aesthetically attractive, environmentally sound, socially inclusive, and gender-responsive trade centers to market these products.

Impact: Increased income among beneficiaries in the selected corridor towns (which are part of the GMS Corridor Towns Development Project) in the three project countries.

Outcome: Increased local employment for poor households

Outputs:
1. Construction of small markets (trade centers) in three project towns completed
2. Microfinance support for market vendors in three project towns
3. Training and awareness campaigns completed 4. Project management, monitoring and audit services established

Business Opportunities
 ▪ Procurement: To be determined

 ▪ Consulting Services: To be determined

Responsible ADB Officer: Florian M. Steinberg (E-mail: ajeffries@adb.org)
 Southeast Asia Department
 Urban Development and Water Division, SERD

TAJIKISTAN

Access to Green Finance Project

Grant No. : 0346
TA No. : 8394
Project No. : 45229-001
Amount (US $ million) : 10
Executing Agencies : **Ministry of Finance**
Sector : **Multisector**

Status: Board approved on 25 June 2013

Description: The project will leverage Tajikistan's sound microfinance system to provide credit for households and microenterprises for energy efficient and environment-friendly homes. The grant will comprise project implementation support of $1.2 million and $8.8 million for 5-year, local currency denominated credit lines to selected microfinance institutions (MFIs). The interest rate on the credit lines will be the NBT refinancing rate, reset annually. An additional technical assistance (TA) grant of $750,000, provided by the Japan Fund for Poverty Reduction (JFPR), will build the capacity of MFIs and the project management unit (PMU) to facilitate efficient green finance intermediation and promote energy efficiency in the country, particularly for rural households and women.

Project Rationale and Linkage to Country/Regional Strategy: Energy challenges coupled with inefficient energy environment. Tajikistan depends on hydroelectric sources for 98% of its electricity needs. In summer, when demand is low but glacial melt is high, there is an electricity surplus. In winter, since rivers freeze, hydroelectric power generation declines by 50%. This results in power outages of up to 18-20 hours per day during winter in grid-connected areas. The situation is worse for the 24,000 households located in remote off-grid areas. Over 73% of the population lives in rural areas and spends much of the winter with limited electricity, with lighting and heating in short supply. In addition, more than 50% (over 500,000 households) of the country's housing units were built in the 1960-1970s. Many of these homes are in rural areas, and their residents include a large number of the 46.7% of families who live below the poverty line. These homes need improvements to increase energy efficiency and reduce household spending on fossil fuels. The problem of energy poverty is complicated by inefficient energy transmission, consumption, and inadequate household understanding about how to use energy in cost-effective, environmentally friendly ways. The United Nations Development Programme (UNDP) estimates that the country's total energy bill was about $1 billion in 2008, which amounted to 20% of the country's gross domestic product that year. This leaves insufficient energy for other productive investment activities, limiting economic growth potential. Rural households depend on fossil and solid fuels such as kerosene, diesel, gasoline, firewood, coal, and manure for their energy needs. Women in these households spend a significant amount of time gathering firewood. Use of these fuels exposes families to health hazards caused by indoor air pollution. Families are unaware of available options to lower energy costs and improve household living conditions.

Pilot interventions by other donors. To tackle some of these challenges, German development cooperation through GIZ and Habitat for Humanity, have undertaken pilot projects. The Warm Comfort program implemented by GIZ has installed thermal insulation and energy efficient solutions in about 200 households in the Gorno-Badakshan region, and plans to scale up. In this program, home improvement solutions for energy efficiency were manufactured and supplied by local cooperatives. The Habitat for Humanity program for home energy efficiency improvements collaborates with two MFIs--IMON and Arvand--for household loans to cover costs for energy efficient roofing and other carpentry works (doors, windows, flooring). The program has so far reached over 6,000 households since 2011. Key lessons learned from both projects are that: (i) home improvements reduce heating requirements up to 40%, resulting to energy savings; (ii) strengthening public awareness of energy efficiency and better energy consumption patterns are necessary; and (iii) MFIs' credit assessment capacity for home improvement loan clients must be strengthened. Both pilot projects cannot expand due to lack of funds, particularly in local currency. Need to upscale and expand pilot interventions. Although small-scale interventions have been initiated by these donors, more than 50% of the country's households are still in need of home improvements for energy efficiency or off-grid clean power generation. A larger-scale intervention with a focus on energy efficiency and environment-friendly solutions--smart green energy solutions (SGES)--can help address the energy challenges that Tajikistan faces. The proposed project will engage the country's microfinance system to provide affordable credit for SGES. SGES can decrease energy consumption by 15% - 50%, enabling these households to consume less fossil fuel. A household survey commissioned by the Asian Development Bank (ADB) also indicated potential demand for solar SGES, with 48% of households expressing interest in acquiring a solar SGES. Some 91% of these households indicated that they would borrow to purchase solar SGES if loans were available.

Provision of better financial access to smart green energy solutions. The project will address the two key barriers limiting effective demand: lack of affordable financing, and insufficient buyer and lender awareness about SGES. The project will provide loans through selected MFIs to households and micro entrepreneurs to purchase and install affordable SGES. Innovative promotion and delivery mechanisms will be used to help make SGES widely acceptable and affordable to low-income households. The project will improve understanding about SGES by increasing public awareness and by providing TA to MFIs. The MFI support will include capacity building and technical advice to MFIs and their clients from SGES experts and engineers who will complete needs assessments, discuss options with clients, and advise on structuring of SGES loans.

Impact: Increased energy efficiency Tajik households

Outcome: Increased access to finance for SGES in Tajikistan

Outputs:
1. Increased outreach by MFIs for green finance, particularly to women borrowers.
2. Increased public awareness of energy efficiency
3. Increased usage of SGES most helpful to women, such as energy-efficient cooking stoves, heating units, and solar water heaters
4. Increased private sector participation

Business Opportunities
- *Consulting Services*: The MOF will recruit 14 individual consultants to staff the PMU. These consultants are: Deputy Head of PMU, Assistant to PMU Head/Office Manager/Translator, Legal Counsel, Monitoring and Evaluation Specialist, Budget, Finance & Credit Manager, Disbursement Specialist, Smart Green Energy Solution Specialist, Organizer/Public Awareness Campaign/Communication Specialist, Due Diligence Specialist, Gender and Social Development Specialist, 2 Office Cleaners, and 2 Drivers. All of the consultants except for the Legal Counsel, monitoring and evaluation, SGES and due diligence specialists, and Office Cleaners will be hired on a full-time basis. Under the JFPR TA, ADB will select a team of individual consultants or a firm to provide a total of 85 person-months of consultancy (66 person-months for national consultants and 19 person-months for international consultants) over the 5-year project implementation period. All consultants will be selected in accordance with the Guidelines on the Use of Consultants by Asian Development Bank and Its Borrowers (2010, as amended from time to time), http://www.adb.org/ documents/guidelines-use-consultants-asian-development-bank-and-its-borrowers.

- *Procurement*: The project's credit lines of $8.8 million (equivalent in Tajik somoni) will be used by rural households (subborrowers) to acquire SGES. Subborrowers may select any supplier of SGES; MFIs may provide subborrowers with a list of potential suppliers. The PMU is expected to acquire 2 vehicles and office equipment and supplies during the first 18 months of the project's implementation period. These goods will be acquired under the Shopping procurement method described in para. 3.5 of ADB's Procurement Guidelines (2010), http://www.adb.org/sites/default/files/Guidelines-Procurement.pdf. Under the Shopping method, the PMU will obtain a minimum of three price quotations.

Responsible ADB Officer: Won Jin Seol (E-mail: wonjinseol@adb.org)
Central and West Asia Department
Public Management, Financial Sector and Trade Division, CWRD

TIMOR-LESTE

District Capital Power Distribution Project

Project No.	:	**44137-022 (Proposed)**
Amount (US $ million)	:	**5.5**
Executing Agencies	:	**Ministry of Infrastructure**
Sector	:	**Energy**

Status: Management Review Meeting scheduled on 16 September 2011

Description: The proposed District Capital Power Distribution Project (the Project) will assist the state-owned power utility, Electricidade de Timor-Leste (EdTL), to rehabilitate existing power distribution infrastructure in five or six district capitals in Timor-Leste. The Project will improve the efficiency, reliability and safety of modern energy services by rehabilitating medium-voltage (MV) and low-voltage (LV) distribution lines and transformers. The Project will upgrade customer grid connections and install prepayment power meters free of charge, thereby improving the revenue collection and commercial viability of EdTL. The Project will build EdTL's asset management capacity and train EdTL in the sustainable operation of power distribution infrastructure. The Project will also build the project implementation capacity of EdTL.

Project Rationale and Linkage to Country/Regional Strategy: Government has prioritized the development of high quality infrastructure as a mainstay of its vision for the country and the importance of the power sector is recognized by the Strategic Development Plan. Government has set a target of 80% electrification by 2025 and has started to address this challenge with a national electrification program. Urgent rehabilitation to improve the efficiency, reliability, and safety of existing power distribution systems is required if district capitals are to share in the full benefits of the extra power to be available as a result of this national program. Support for infrastructure has been a feature of ADB's country strategy and the energy sector has been identified as a priority sector in the most recent Country Partnership Strategy. The Project is included in the latest Country Operations Business Plan and government has welcomed ADB assistance for power distribution.

Impact: Increased access to energy in district capitals

Outcome: EdTL distributes electric power efficiently, reliably and safely in the project areas

Outputs:
1. The power distribution network is rehabilitated by EdTL in the project areas
2. Sustainable management of power distribution assets by EdTL
3. Customers are aware of the importance of energy conservation
4. Effective project management capacity is established in EdTL

<u>Business Opportunities</u>
- Consulting Services: To be determined

- Procurement: To be determined

Responsible ADB Officer: Robert Kesterton (E-mail: rkesterton@adb.org)
Pacific Department
Transport, Energy and Natural Resources Division, PARD

TONGA

Outer Island Renewable Energy Project

Grant No.	:	**0347, 0348**
Project No.	:	**43452-022**
Amount (US $ million)	:	**2**
Executing Agencies	:	**Ministry of Finance and National Planning**
Sector	:	**Energy**

Status: Board approved on 27 June 2013

Description: The proposed Tonga Outer Island Renewable Energy Project (the Project) will construct grid-connected Solar Photovoltaic (PV) power plants on the outer islands of Tonga, thereby demonstrating a method for reducing the country's heavy reliance on imported fossil fuels for power generation. The Project will supply secure, environmentally sustainable energy to households, schools, and other public facilities, on the islands of 'Eua, Ha'apai, and Vava'u. The Project will quantify the solar resource and facilitate the integration of intermittent renewable energy with a conventional diesel grid. The Project will build the capacity of the power utility, Tonga Power Limited (TPL), in the operation and maintenance of renewable technologies. Customers will be made aware of the importance of energy conservation and opportunities for passing cost savings to poor households by way of a subsidized tariff will be assessed during project preparation.

Project Rationale and Linkage to Country/Regional Strategy: The government of Tonga set a target of reducing fossil fuel imports for power generation by 50% by 2020 and has developed an overall plan for the energy sector. The Tonga Energy Roadmap 2010-2020 outlines the improvements needed to reach the government's 2020 target, and covers petroleum supply chain initiatives, energy efficiency, and renewable energy technologies. The Roadmap was developed in very close collaboration with development partners and has been held up at regional meetings as an example of donor coordination. This project is identified as a high priority by the Roadmap and the Roadmap Implementation Unit has requested assistance with this project from ADB. Demarcation of this project has also been enhanced through discussions with government concerning the country partnership strategy and country operations business plan.

Impact: Tonga's dependence on imported fossil fuel for power generation is reduced.

Outcome: TPL introduces the supply of clean, reliable power in the outer islands

Outputs:
1. TPL installs Solar PV power generating technology in the outer islands
2. Sustainable management of grid-connected renewable energy by TPL
3. Customers are aware of the importance of energy conservation
4. Effective project implementation is established and demonstrated

Business Opportunities
- Consulting Services: To be determined

- Procurement: To be determined

Responsible ADB Officer: Paul Hattle (E-mail: phattle@adb.org)
Pacific Department
Transport, Energy and Natural Resources Division, PARD

V. IN-COUNTRY EMBASSY AND COMMERCIAL OFFICES

COUNTRY	EMBASSY POST	COMMERCIAL POST
Afghanistan	American Embassy, Kabul The Great Masoud Road between Radio Afghanistan & Ministry of Public Health, Kabul, Afghanistan Tel.: (93-20) 130-0436; Fax: (93-20) 130-1364 *James B. Cunningham, Ambassador*	c/o American Embassy, Kabul The Great Masoud Road between Radio Afghanistan & Ministry of Public Health, Kabul, Afghanistan Tel.: (93) 070-108-364 *Mr. Greg Lawless, Political/Economic Officer* E-mail: LawlessGF@state.gov; KabulEcon@state.gov *Mr. Charles P. Siner, Economic Officer* E-mail: SinerC@state/gov
Armenia	Embassy of the United States of America 1 American Avenue Yerevan 0082, Republic of Armenia Tel.: (374 10) 464-700; Fax:(374 10) 464-742 E-mail: usinfo@usa.am *John A. Heffern, Ambassador*	Embassy of the United States of America 18 Marshal Bagramian Ave. Yerevan 375019, Republic of Armenia Tel.: (374 10) 464-701; Fax:(374 10) 464-742 *Mr. Brian Roraff, Political-Economic Section Chief* E-mail: RoraffBR@state.gov
Australia *Canberra*	U.S. Embassy Moonah Place, Yarralumla Canberra, Australia Tel.: (61-2) 6214 5600; Fax: (61-2) 6214 5970 *Jeffrey L. Bleich, Ambassador*	U.S. Commercial Service c/o U.S. Consulate General, Sydney Tel.: (61-2) 9373-9205; Fax: (61-2) 9221-0573 *Mr. Joe Kaesshaefer, Senior Commercial Officer* E-mail: Joe.Kaesshaefer@trade.gov
Melbourne	U.S. Consulate General 553 St., Kilda Road Melbourne, VIC 3004 Tel.: (61-03) 9526-5900; Fax: (61-03) 9510-4646 *Frank C. Urbancic, Consul General*	U.S. Commercial Service c/o U.S. Consulate General, Melbourne 553 St., Kilda Road, Melbourne, VIC 3004 Tel.: (61-3) 9526-5927; Fax: (61-3) 9510-4660 *Ms. Annette Ahern, Commercial Specialist* E-mail: Annette.Ahern@trade.gov
Sydney	U.S. Consulate General MLC Centre, Level 59 19-29 Martin Place Sydney NSW 2000, Australia Tel.: (61-2) 9373-9200; Fax: (61-2) 9373-9125 *Niels Marquardt, Consul General*	U.S. Commercial Service c/o U.S. Consulate General, Sydney MLC Centre, Level 59 19-29 Martin Place, Sydney NSW 2000, Australia Tel.: (61-2) 9373-9205; Fax: (61-2) 9221-0573 *Mr. Joe Kaesshaefer, Senior Commercial Officer* E-mail: Joe.Kaesshaefer@trade.gov *Mr. Duncan Archibald, Commercial Specialist* E-mail: Duncan.Archibald@trade.gov

COUNTRY	EMBASSY POST	COMMERCIAL POST
Azerbaijan	U.S. Embassy 83 Azadliq Prospekti Baku , Azerbaijan 370007 Tel.: (994-12) 980-335 to 37 Fax: (994-12) 656-671 *Richard L. Morningstar, Ambassador*	Foreign Commercial Service US Department of State (Baku) Washington DC 20521-7050 Tel.: (994-12) 498-0335; Fax: (994-12) 986-117 *Mr. Robert Garverick, Political/Economic Officer* E-mail: GarverickJR@state.gov
Bangladesh	U.S. Embassy Madani Avenue, Baridhara Dhaka 1212, Bangladesh Tel.: (880) 885-5500; Fax: (880) 882-3744 *Dan W. Mozena, Ambassador*	U.S. Embassy Madani Avenue, Baridhara Dhaka 1212, Bangladesh Tel.: (880) 885-5500; Fax: (880) 882-3744 *Prof. Asif Ayub, State Commercial Specialist* E-mail: AyubAX@state.gov
Bhutan	c/o U.S. Embassy Shanti Path Chanakyapuri New Delhi 110021, India Tel.: (91-11) 2419-8000; Fax: (91-11) 2419-0017 *Timothy J. Roemer, Ambassador*	c/o U.S. Commercial Service, New Delhi 24 Kasturba Gandhi Marg New Delhi 110001, India Tel.: (91-11) 2331-6841/48; Fax: (91-11) 2331-5172 *Mr. Richard Craig, Principal Commercial Officer* E-mail: Richard.Craig@trade.gov *Mr. Richard Rothman, Senior Commercial Officer* E-mail: Richard.Rothman@trade.gov *Ms. Margaret Hanson-Muse, Deputy Senior Commercial Officer* E-mail: Margaret.Hanson-Muse@trade.gov Economic/Commercial Section U.S. Embassy
Brunei	U.S. Embassy Spg 336-52-16-9, Jln Kebangsaan BC4115 Negara, Brunei Darussalam Tel.: (673) 238-4616; Fax: (673) 238-4603 E-mail: amembassy_bsb@state.gov *Daniel L. Shields, Ambassador*	Spg 336-52-16-9, Jln Kebangsaan BC4115 Negara, Brunei Darussalam Tel.: (673) 238-4616; Fax: (673) 238-4603 *Matthew B. Stannard, Political/ Economic Officer* E-mail: stannardmb@state.gov
Cambodia	U.S. Embassy, Phnom Penh #1, Street 96, Sangkat Wat Phnom Phnom Penh, Cambodia Tel.: (855) 23 728-000 Fax: (855-23) 728-600 *Mr. William E. Todd, Ambassador*	Economic/Commercial Section U.S. Embassy, Phnom Penh #1, Street 96 Phnom Penh, Cambodia Tel.: (855) 23-728-137; Fax: (855-23) 728-888 *Mr. David Myers, Political/ Econ Officer* E-mail: MyersDR3@state.gov *Sokros Chann, Commercial Specialist* E-mail: channs@state.gov

COUNTRY	EMBASSY POST	COMMERCIAL POST
China **Beijing**	U.S. Embassy No. 55 An Jia Lou Road, Beijing 100600, China Tel.: (86-10) 6532-3831; Fax: (86-10) 6532-6929 *Gary F. Locke, Ambassador*	U.S. Commercial Service 31/F, North Tower Beijing Kerry Center, No. 1 Guanghua Lu, Beijing 100020, China Tel.: (86-10) 8529-6655; Fax: (86-10) 8529-6558/6559 *Mr. David Murphy, Commercial Officer* E-mail: David.Murphy@trade.gov *Ms. Elizabeth Shieh, Commercial Officer* E-mail: Elizabeth.Shieh@trade.gov *Ms. Yue Cao, Senior Commercial Specialist* E-mail: Yue.Cao@trade.gov
Chengdu	U.S. Consulate General 4 Lingshiguan Lu, Renmin Nanlu Sec. 4, Chengdu, Sichuan 610041, China Tel.: (86-28) 8558-3992; 8558-9642 Fax: (86-28) 8558-3520 E-mail: consularchengdu@state.gov *Peter Haymond, Consul General*	U.S. Commercial Service 4 Lingshiguan Lu, Renmin Nanlu, Section 4, Chengdu, Sichuan 610041, China Tel: (86-28) 8558-3992; Fax: (86-28) 8558-9221 *Mr. William Marshak, Principal Commercial Officer* E-mail: William.Marshak@trade.gov *Ms. Lin Liping, Senior Commercial Specialist* E-mail: Lin.Liping@trade.gov
Guangzhou	U.S. Consulate General #1 Shamian South St., Guangzhou 510133, PRC Tel.: (86-20) 8121-8000; Fax: (86-20) 8121-6296 *Jennifer Zimdahl Galt, Consul General*	U.S. Commercial Service 14/F, China Hotel Office Tower, Room 1461 Li Hua Road, Guangzhou 510015, China Tel.: (86-20) 8667-4011; Fax: (86-20) 8666-6409 *Mr. Gregory Wong, Principal Commercial Officer* E-mail: Greg.Wong@trade.gov *Ms. Diana Liu, Senior Commercial Specialist* E-mail: Diana.Liu@trade.gov
Shanghai	U.S.Consulate General 1469 Huai Hai Zhong Lu Shanghai 200031, PRC Tel.: (86-21) 6433-3936; Fax: (86-21) 6433-4122 *Robert Griffiths, Consul General*	U.S. Commercial Service Shanghai Center, Suite 631 1376 Nanjing West Road, Shanghai 200040, China Tel.: (86-21) 6279-7630; Fax: (86-21) 6279-7639 *Mr. William Brekke, Principal Commercial Officer* E-mail: William.Brekke@trade.gov *Ms. Stellar Chu, Senior Commercial Specialist* E-mail: Stellar.Chu@trade.gov
Shenyang	U.S. Consulate General No. 52, 14 Wei Road, Heping District Shenyang, Liaoning 110003, China Tel.: (86-24) 2322-1198; Fax: (86-24) 2322-1942 E-mail: shenyangacs@state.gov *Sean Stein, Consul General*	U.S. Commercial Service No. 52, 14 Wei Road, Heping District Shenyang, Liaoning 110003, China Tel.: (86-24) 2322-1198; Fax: (86-24) 2322-2206 *Ms. Yang Liu, Commercial Specialist* E-mail: Cathy.Feig@trade.gov *Ms. June Xu, Commercial Specialist* E-mail: June.Xu@trade.gov

COUNTRY	EMBASSY POST	COMMERCIAL POST
Cook Islands	c/o U.S. Embassy Moonah Place, Yarralumla Canberra, Australia Tel.: (61-62) 6214 5600; Fax: (61-62) 6214 5970 *Jeffrey L. Bleich, Ambassador*	c/o U.S. Commercial Service, Sydney U.S. Consulate General MLC Centre, Level 59 19-29 Martin Place Sydney NSW 2000, Australia Tel.: (61-2) 9373-9205; Fax: (612) 9221-0573 *Mr. Joe Kaesshaefer, Senior Commercial Officer* E-mail: Joe.Kaesshaefer@trade.gov
Fiji Islands	U.S. Embassy 158 Princes Road, Tamavua, Suja, Fiji Tel.: (679) 3314-466; Fax: (679) 330-5106 E-mail: usembsuva@is.com.fj *Mr. Frankie A. Reed, Ambassador*	Commercial Section, U.S. Embassay Suva 158 Princes Road, Tamavua, Suja, Fiji Tel.: (679) 3314-466; Fax: (679) 330-5106 *Michael Via, Economics Officer* (E-mail: ViaMA@state.gov)
Georgia	U.S. Embassy 11 George Balanchine Street, Tbilisi, Georgia, 0131 Tel.: (995 32) 2770 00; Fax: (995 32) 532310 *Richard Norland, Ambassador*	c/o U.S. Embassy 11 George Balanchine Street, Tbilisi, Digomi, Georgia, 0131 Tel.: (995 32) 2770 00; Fax: (995 32) 532310 *Alan Meltzer, Political Chief* E-mail: MeltzerAD@state.gov
Hong Kong	U.S. Consulate General 26 Garden Road, Hong Kong, SAR, China Tel.: (852) 2523-9011; Fax: (852) 2845-1598 *Stephen M. Young, Consul General*	American Consulate General U.S. Consulate General 26 Garden Road, Central Hong Kong, SAR, China Tel.: (852) 2521-5752; Fax: (852) 2845-9800 *Mr. Charles Wall, Commercial Officer* E-mail: Charles.Wall@trade.gov *Ms. Olevia Yim, Senior Commercial Specialist* E-mail: Olevia.Yim@trade.gov
India *Ahmedabad*	c/o U.S. Consulate General, Mumbai Lincoln House, Bhulabhai Desai Road, Mumbai 400 026, India Tel.: (91-22) 2363-3611; Fax: (91-22) 2363-0350 *Timothy J. Roemer, Ambassador*	U.S. Commercial Service JMC House, Suite 401/402, Opp. Parimal Garden, Ambawadi Ahmedabad 380 006, Gujarat Tel.: (91-79) 2656-5210/ 2656 5216; Fax: (91-79) 2656-0763 *Ms. Sangeeta Taneja, Commercial Specialist* E-mail: Sangeeta.Taneja@trade.gov
Bangalore	c/o U.S. Consulate General, Chennai 220 Anna Salai, Gemini Circle Chennai 600 006, India Tel.: (91-44) 2857 4242; Fax: (91-44) 2811-2020 *Andrew T. Simkin, Consul General*	U.S. Commercial Service S2, 2nd Floor, Red Cross Bhavan 26, Race Course Road, Bangalore 560 001, India Tel.: (91-80) 2220-6401; Fax: (91-80) 2220-6405 *Mr. Leonard Roberts, Senior Commercial Specialist* E-mail: Leonard.Roberts@trade.gov

COUNTRY	EMBASSY POST	COMMERCIAL POST
India *Chennai*	U.S. Consulate General 220 Anna Salai, Gemini Circle Chennai 600 006, India Tel.: (91-44) 2811-4000; Fax: (91-44) 2811-2020 *Ms. Jennifer McIntyre, Consul General*	U.S. Commercial Service U.S. Consulate General 220 Anna Salai, Gemini Circle Chennai 600 006, India Tel.: (91-44) 2857-4059; Fax: (91-44) 2857-4212 *Mr. James P. Golsen, Principal Commercial Officer* E-mail: Vaidyanathan.Purushothaman@trade.gov *Mr. Vaidyanathan Purushothaman, Senior Commercial Specialist* E-mail: Vaidyanathan.Purushothaman@trade.gov
Hyderabad	U.S. Consulate General Paigah Palace 1-8-323, Chiran Fort Lane, Begumpet, Secunderabad 500 003, India Tel.: (91-40) 4033-8300; Fax: (91-40) 4033-8301 *Katherine S. Dhanani, Consul General*	U.S. Commercial Service # 555, "E" level Taj Deccan Road No. 1 Banjara Hills Hyderabad 500 034 Tel.: (91-40) 2330-5000; Fax: (91-40) 2330-0130 *Mr. Pandrangi Radhakishore, Commercial Specialist* E-mail: Pandrangi.Radhakishore@trade.gov
Kolkata	U.S. Consulate General 5/1 Ho Chi Minh Sarani Kolkata 700 071, India Tel.: (91-33) 3984 2400; Fax: (91-33) 2282-2335 *Dean R. Thompson, Consul General*	U.S. Commercial Service American Center 38-A, Jawaharlal Nehru Road, Kolkata (Calcutta) 700 071 Tel.: (91-33) 2288-1200; Fax: (91-33) 2288-1207 *Mr. Richard Craig, Principal Commercial Officer* E-mail: Richard.Craig@trade.gov *Mr. Arup Mitra, Commercial Specialist* E-mail: Arup.Mitra@trade.gov
Mumbai	U.S. Consulate General Lincoln House 78, Bhulabhai Desai Road, Mumbai 400 026, India Tel.: (91-22) 2363-3611; Fax: (91-22) 2363-0350 *Mr. Peter Haas, Consul General*	U.S. Commercial Service American Center 4 New Marine Lines Mumbai 400 020, India Tel.: (91-22) 2265-2511; Fax: (91-22) 2262-3850 *Mr. Richard Rothman, Senior Commercial Officer* E-mail: Richard.Rothman@trade.gov *Ms. Marsha McDaniel, Commercial Officer* E-mail: Marsha.McDaniel@trade.gov *Mr. P Srinivas, Senior Commercial Specialist* E-mail: P.Srinivas@trade.gov *Mr. Sanjay Arya, Commercial Specialist* E-mail: Sanjay.Arya@trade.gov

COUNTRY	EMBASSY POST	COMMERCIAL POST
India *New Delhi*	U.S. Embassy Shanti Path, Chanakyapuri New Delhi, 110 021 Tel.: (91-11) 2419-8000; Fax: (91-11) 2419-0017 *Nancy J. Powell, Ambassador*	U.S. Commercial Service The American Center, 24 Kasturba Gandhi Marg New Delhi 110 001, India Tel.: (91-11) 234 72000; Fax: (91-11) 2331 5172 *Ms. Margaret Hanson-Muse, Deputy Senior Commercial Officer* E-mail: Margaret.Hanson-Muse@trade.gov *Mr. Gregory O'Connor, Commercial Officer* E-mail: Greg.O'Connor@trade.gov *Mr. Thomas P. Cassidy, Commercial Officer* E-mail: Pat.Cassidy@trade.gov *Mr. Sandeep Maini, Senior Commercial Specialist* E-mail: Sandeep.Maini@trade.gov
Indonesia *Jakarta*	U.S. Embassy JI, Merdeke Selatan, No. 3-5 Jakarta 10110 Indonesia Tel.: (62-21) 3435-9000; Fax: (62-21) 385-7189 *Scot Marciel, Ambassador*	U.S. Commercial Service Wisma Metropolitan II 3/F JI., Jendral Sudirman Kav. 29-31 Jakarta 12920, Indonesia Tel.: (62-21) 526-2850 Ext 3001; Fax: (62-21) 526-2855 *Mr. David Gossack, Principal Commercial Officer* E-mail: David.Gossack@trade.gov *Mr. Jesse Lapierre, Commercial Officer* E-mail: Jesse.Lapierre@trade.gov *Ms. Anasia Silviati, Senior Commercial Specialist* E-mail: Anasia.Silviati@trade.gov *Mr. Kalung Riang, Commercial Specialist* E-mail: Kalung.Riang@trade.gov
Japan *Tokyo*	U.S. Embassy 10-5 Akasaka 1-chome, Minato-ku Tokyo 107-8420 Japan Tel.: (81-03) 3224 5000; Fax: (81-03) 3505 1862 *John V. Roos, Ambassador*	U.S. Embassy U.S. Commercial Service 1-10-5 Akasaka Minato-ku Tokyo 107-8420 Japan Tel.: (81-3) 3224-5050; Fax: (81-3) 3589-4235 *Mr. Andrew Wylegala, Senior Commercial Officer* E-mail: Andrew.Wylegala@trade.gov *Mr. Tomohiro Asakawa, Senior Commercial Specialist* E-mail: Tomohiro.Asakawa@trade.gov
Kazakhstan	U.S. Embassy Ak Bulak 4, Str. 23-22, building #3, Astana 010010, Kazakhstan Tel.: +7 (7172) 70-21-00; Fax: +7 (7172) 34-08-90 *Kenneth J. Fairfax, Ambassador*	U.S. Commercial Service, 41 Kazibek bi St. 050010, Almaty, Kazakhstan Tel.: (7-327) 250-4920; Fax: (7-327) 250-4967 Email: almaty.office.box@mail.doc.gov *Ms. Azhar Kadrzhanova, Commercial Specialist* E-mail: Azhar.Kadrzhanova@trade.gov *Mr. Nurlan Zhangarin, Commercial Specialist* E-mail: Nurlan.Zhangarin@trade.gov

COUNTRY	EMBASSY POST	COMMERCIAL POST
Kiribati	c/o U.S. Embassy, Majuro Mejen Weto, Oceanside, Majuro, Republic of the Marshall Islands Tel.: (692) 247-4011; Fax: (692) 247-4012 *Ms. Martha Campbell, Ambassador*	c/o U.S. Embassy, Majuro Oceanside Mejen Weto, Long Island Majuro, Republic of the Marshall Islands Tel.: (692) 247-4011; Fax: (692) 247-4012 *Andrew Zvirzdin, Political/Economic Officer* E-mail: ZvirzdinAJ@state.gov
Korea (South)	U.S. Embassy 188 Sejong-daero, Jongno-gu, Seoul 110-710, South Korea Tel.: (82-2) 397-4114; Fax: (82-2) 738-8845 *Sung Y. Kim, Ambassador*	U.S. Commercial Service U.S. Embassy, Seoul 188 Sejong-daero, Jongno-gu, Seoul 110-710 Korea Tel.: (82-2) 397-4114; Fax: (82-2) 738-8845 *Mr. Keenton Chiang, Commercial Officer* E-mail: Keenton.Chiang@trade.gov *Ms. Yoon Shil Chay, Senior Commercial Specialist* E-mail: YoonShil.Chay@trade.gov
Kyrgyz Republic	U.S. Embassy 171 Prospect Mira 720016, Bishkek Tel.: (996-312) 551-241 Fax: (996-312) 551-264 *Pamela L. Spratlen, Ambassador*	Commercial Section U.S. Embassy 171 Prospect Mira 720016, Bishkek Tel.: (996-312) 551-241 Ext. 4403 Fax: (996-312) 551-264 *Mr. David McCormick, Economic/Political Officer* E-mail: McCormickDL@state.gov
Laos	U.S. Embassy 19 Rue Bartholonie Vientiane, Lao P.D.R. Tel.: (856) 212-67000; Fax: (856) 212-67190 *Karen B. Stewart, Ambassador*	Economic Section, U.S. Embassy 19 Rue Bartholonie Vientiane, Lao P.D.R. Tel.: (856) 212-67156; Fax: (856) 212-67074 *Mr. Matthew Younger, Economic and Commercial Officer* E-mail: youngermb@state.gov *Mr. Dustin Bickel* (E-mail: BickelD@state.gov) *Ms. Sivanphone Thoummabout, Econ/Commercial Assistant* E-mail: SivanphoneTX@state.gov
Malaysia	U.S. Embassy 376 Jalan Tun Razak 50400 Kuala Lumpur, Malaysia Tel.: (60-3) 2168-5000; Fax: (60-3) 2142-2207 *Paul W. Jones, Ambassador*	U.S. Commercial Service U.S. Embassy 376 Jalan Tun Razak 50700 Kuala Lumpur, Malaysia Tel.: (60-3) 2168-5000; Fax: (60-3) 2142-1866 *Mr. Stephen Jacques, Senior Commercial Officer* E-mail: Stephen.Jacques@trade.gov *Ms. Umaranjine Arumugam, Commercial Specialist* E-mail: Umaranjine.Arumugam@trade.gov
Maldives	c/o U.S. Embassy 210 Galle Road Colombo 3, Sri Lanka Tel.: (9411) 2448-007; Fax: (9411) 247-1092 *Michele Sison, Ambassador*	c/o U.S. Embassy 210 Galle Road, Colombo 3, Sri Lanka Tel.: (94 11) 249-8770; Fax: (94 11) 249-8820 *Ms. Allison V. Areias, Economic Officer* E-mail: AreiasAV@state.gov

COUNTRY	EMBASSY POST	COMMERCIAL POST
Marshall Islands	U.S. Embassy Oceanside Mejen Weto, Long Island, Majuro Republic of the Marshall Islands Tel.: (692) 247-4011; Fax: (692) 247-4012 *Ms. Martha Campbell, Ambassador*	U.S. Embassy, Majuro PO Box 1379, Oceanside Mejen Weto, Long Island, Majuro Republic of the Marshall Islands Tel.: (692) 247-4011; Fax: (692) 247-4012 *Andrew Zvirzdin, Political/Economic Officer* E-mail: ZvirzdinAJ@state.gov
Micronesia, Federal States of	U.S. Embassy 4120 Kolonia Place Washington, D.C. 20521-4120 Tel.: (691) 3202-187; Fax: (691) 3202-186 *Dorothea-Maria (Doria) Rosen, Ambassador* E-mail: USEmbassy@mail.fm	U.S. Embassy P.O. Box 1286 Kolonia, Pohnpei 96941 FSM Tel.: (691) 320-8195; Fax: (691) 3202-186 *Charles Thomas, Economic Officer* E-mail: ThomasCA2@state.gov
Mongolia	U.S. Embassy Big Ring Road, 11th Microdistrict, Sukhbaatar District, Ulaanbaatar 13, Mongolia Tel.: (976-11) 329-095; Fax: (976-11) 320-776 E-mail: receptionist@usembassy.mn *Jonathan Addleton, Ambassador*	Commercial Section U.S. Embassy P.O. Box 1021 Ulaanbaatar 13, Mongolia Tel.: (976-11) 329-095; Fax: (976-11) 320-776 *David Wyche, Economic/ Commercial Officer* E-mail: WycheDL@state.gov *Michael Richmond, Senior Commercial Specialist* E-mail: RichmondMD@state.gov
Myanmar (Burma)	U.S.Embassy - Burma The 110 University Avenue, Kamayut Township Rangoon, Burma Tel.: (95 1) 536509; Fax: (95 1) 511069 *Derek Mitchell, Ambassador*	U.S.Embassy - Burma The 110 University Avenue, Kamayut Township Rangoon, Burma Tel.: (95 1) 536509; Fax: (95 1) 511069 Michael Mcgee, Regional Senior Commercial Officer Commercial Service Thailand *Machut Shishak, Economics Officer* E-mail: ShishakMA@state.gov
Nauru	c/o U.S. Embassy 31 Loftus Street, Suva, Fiji P.O. Box 218 Suva, Fiji Tel.: (679) 3314-466; Fax: (679) 3308-685 E-mail: usembsuva@is.com.fj *Mr. Frankie A. Reed, Ambassador*	c/o U.S. Embassy 31 Loftus Street, P.O. Box 218, Suva Fiji Tel.: (679) 3314-466; Fax: (679) 3308-685 Michael Via, Economics Officer (E-mail: ViaMA@state.gov)
Nepal	U.S. Embassy Maharajgunj, Kathmandu, Nepal Tel.: (977-1) 400-7200; Fax: (977-1) 400-7272 *Patricia Mahoney, Chargé d'Affaires*	Commercial Section U.S. Embassy Pani Pokhari, Kathmandu Tel.: (977-1) 4411-179; Fax: (977-1) 4419-963 *Mr. Michael Goldman, Political/ Economic Officer* E-mail: GoldmanMB@state.gov *Mr.Timothy Trenkle* E-mail: TrenkleTP@state.gov

COUNTRY	EMBASSY POST	COMMERCIAL POST
New Zealand	U.S. Embassy 29 Fitzherbert Terrace, Thorndorn Wellington, New Zealand Tel.: (64-4) 462-6000; Fax: (64-4) 472-3478 E-mail: wellington.arc@state.gov *David Huebner, Ambassador*	U.S. Commercial Service American Embassy 29 Fitzherbert Terrace, Thorndorn Wellington, New Zealand Tel.: (644) 462-6002; Fax: (644) 473-0770 *Colin Crosby, Political/ Economic Officer* E-mail: CrosbyCT2@state.gov *Ms. Janet Coulthart, Commercial Specialist* E-mail: Janet.Coulthart@trade.gov
Pakistan *Islamabad*	U.S. Embassy Diplomatic Enclave, Ramna 5 Islamabad, Pakistan Tel.: (92-51) 2080000; Fax: (92-51) 2276-427 *Richard E. Hoagland, Chargé d'affaires*	U.S. Commercial Service American Embassy, Diplomatic Enclave Ramna-5, Islamabad, Pakistan Tel.: 011-92-51-2080-2530; Fax: 011-92-51-282-3981 *Mr. James Fluker, Commercial Officer* E-mail: James.Fluker@trade.gov *Mr. Tariq Sayeed, Senior Commercial Specialist* E-mail: Tariq.Sayeed@trade.gov
Karachi	U.S. Consulate General 8, Abdullah Haroon Road Karachi 75530, Pakistan Tel.: (92-21) 3520-4200; Fax: (92-21) 3568-0496 *Michael Dodman, Consul General*	U.S. Commercial Service 3, 4, 5, New TPX Area, Mai Kolachi Road, Karachi, Pakistan. Tel.: 011-92-21-568-5170; Fax: 01192-21-568-1749 *Mr. Malik Attiq, Commercial Specialist* E-mail: Malik.Attiq@trade.gov
Lahore	U.S. Consulate General 50, Shahrah-e-Abdul Hameed Bin Badees, near Shimla Hill, Lahore, Pakistan Tel.: (92-42) 3603-4000; Fax: (92-42) 3603-4200 *Ms. Nina Maria Fite, Consul General*	U.S. Commercial Service U.S. Consulate General 50 Shahrah-E-Bin Badees Lahore, Pakistan *Mr. Aftab Qamar, Commercial Specialist* E-mail: Aftab.Qamar@trade.gov
Peshawar	U.S. Consulate General 11, Hospital Road Peshawar Cantonment, Pakistan Tel.: (92-91) 526 8800; 285-496/97 Fax: (92-91) 5276712 & 5284171 *Robert Reed, Consul General*	
Palau *Koror*	U.S. Embassy P.O. Box 6028, Koror PW 96940 Tel.: 680-488-2920/2990; Fax: 680-488-2911 E-mail: USembassyKoror@palaunet.com *Helen P. Reed-Rowe, Ambassador*	U.S. Embassy P.O. Box 6028, Koror PW 96940 Tel.: 680-488-2920/2991; Fax: 680-488-2912 *Les Jocelyn Isechal, Political Officer* E-mail: IsechalJ@state.gov

COUNTRY	EMBASSY POST	COMMERCIAL POST
Papua New Guinea	U.S. Embassy Douglas Street, Port Moresby Papua New Guinea P.O. Box 1492 Port Moresby NCD, Papua New Guinea Tel.: (675) 321-1455; Fax: (675) 320-0637 *Teddy B. Taylor, Ambassador* E-mail: png@state.gov	Commercial Section c/o U.S. Embassy, Port Moresby P.O. Box 1492 Port Moresby NCD, Papua New Guinea Tel.: (675) 321-1455 ext. 2136; Fax: (675) 320-0637 *Mr. Regis Prevot, Economic/Political Officer* E-mail: PrevotRE@state.gov
Philippines	U.S. Embassy 1201 Roxas Blvd., Ermita 1000 Manila Tel.: (63-2) 301-2000; Fax: (63-2) 301-2668 *Mr. Harry Thomas, Ambassador*	U.S. Commercial Service American Business Center Ayala Life– FGU Center 25/F, 6811 Ayala Avenue, Makati City 1226 Metro Manila Tel.: (63-2) 888-6080; Fax: (63-2) 888-6606 *Mr. James McCarthy, Senior Commercial Officer* E-mail: James.McCarthy@trade.gov *Tyrena Holley, Commercial Officer* E-mail: Tyrena.Holley@trade.gov
Samoa	U.S Embassy 5th Floor, Accident Corporation Building, Matafele, Apia, Samoa Tel.: (685) +685 21436 / 21631 / 21452 or 22696 Fax: (685) 22-030 *David Huebner, Ambassador* E-mail: usembassy@samoa.net	U.S. Commercial Service American Embassy 29 Fitzherbert Terrace, Thorndorn Wellington, New Zealand Tel.: (644) 462-6002; Fax: (644) 473-0770 *Mr. Joe Kaesshaefer, Senior Commercial Officer* E-mail: Joe.Kaesshaefer@trade.gov *Ms. Janet Coulthart, Commercial Specialist* E-mail: Janet.Coulthart@trade.gov
Singapore	U.S Embassy 27 Napier Road, Singapore 258508 Tel.: (65) 6476-9100; Fax: (65) 6476-9340 *David I. Adelman, Ambassador*	U.S. Commercial Service U.S. Embassy 27 Napier Road, Singapore Tel.: (65) 6476-9037; 6476-9041; Fax: (65) 6476-9080 *Ms. Sweehoon Chia, Senior Commercial Specialist* E-mail: Sweehoon.Chia@trade.gov
Solomon Islands	c/o U.S. Embassy - Port Moresby Douglas Street, Port Moresby Papua New Guinea P.O. Box 1492 Port Moresby NCD, Papua New Guinea Tel.: (675) 321-1455; Fax: (675)320-0637 *Teddy B. Taylor, Ambassador*	Commercial Section c/o U.S. Embassy, Port Moresby P.O. Box 1492 Port Moresby NCD, Papua New Guinea Tel.: (675) 321-1455; Fax: (675) 320-0637 *Mr. Regis Prevot, Economic/Political Officer* E-mail: PrevotRE@state.gov

COUNTRY	EMBASSY POST	COMMERCIAL POST
Sri Lanka	U.S. Embassy 210 Galle Road Colombo 3, Sri Lanka Tel.: (9411) 2448-007; Fax: (9411) 243-7345 *Ambassador Michele Sison, Ambassador*	Commercial Section U.S. Embassy 210 Galle Road, Colombo 3, Sri Lanka Tel.: (9411) 2448-007; Fax: (9411) 247-1092 *Ms, Allison V. Areias, Economic Officer* E-mail: AreiasAV@state.gov
Taiwan	American Institute in Taiwan 5F, #2 Chung Cheng 3rd Road, Taiwan Tel.: (886-2) 2162-2000; Fax: (886-2) 2162-2251 *Christopher J. Marut, Director* E-mail: aitarc@mail.ait.org.tw	U.S. Commercial Service American Institute in Taiwan 2 Chung Cheng 3rd Road 5F Kaohsiung *Ms. Helen Hwang, Senior Commercial Officer* Tel: 011-886-7-238-7744; Fax: 011-886-7-238-5237 E-mail: Helen.Hwang@trade.gov
Tajikistan	U.S. Embassy 109-A Ismoili Somoni Avenue (Zarafshon district) Dushanbe, Tajikistan 734019 Tel.: [992] (37) 229 20 00 Fax: [992] (37) 229 20 50, 236 04 30 *Sarah Penhune, Chargé d'Affaires, a.i.*	c/o U.S. Embassy - Dushanbe 10 Pavlov Street Dushanbe 734003 Tajikistan Tel.: (992-372) 292501 Fax: (992-372) 210362; 510028 *Benjamin J. Gibson, Economic Officer* E-mail: GibsonBJ@state.gov
Thailand *Bangkok* *Chiang Mai*	U.S. Embassy 120-122 Wireless Road Bangkok, Thailand 10330 Tel.: (66-2) 205-4000; Fax: (66-2) 205-4131 *Kristie A. Kenney, Ambassador* U.S. Consulate General 387 Wichayanond Road Chiang Mai 50300, Thailand Tel.: (66-53) 107-700; Fax: (66-53) 252-633 *Kenneth L. Foster, Consul General*	U.S. Commercial Service GPF Witthayu, Tower A, Suite 302 93/1 Wireless Road, Pathumwan, Bangkok 10330, Thailand Tel.: 662-205-5090; Fax: 662-255-2915 *Mr. Michael L. McGee, Regional Senior Commercial Officer* E-mail: Michael.McGee@trade.gov *Ms. Wanwemol Charukultharvatch, Senior Commercial Specialist* E-mail: Wanwemol.Charukultharvatch@trade.gov *Ms. Kornluck Tantisaeree, Commercial Specialist* E-mail: Kornluck.Tantisaeree@trade.gov
Timor-Leste	U.S. Embassy Avenida de Portugal, Praia dos Coqueiros, Dili, Timor-Leste Tel.: (670) 332-4684; Fax: (670) 331-3206 *Judith Fergin, Ambassador*	U.S. Embassy Avenida de Portugal, Praia dos Coqueiros Dili, Timor-Leste Tel.: (670) 332-4684 ext. 2034 Fax: (670) 331-3206 *Mr. Jeff Borenstein, Political/Economic Officer* E-mail: BorensteinJD@state.gov

COUNTRY	EMBASSY POST	COMMERCIAL POST
Tonga	c/o U.S. Embassy 31 Loftus Street Suva, Fiji Tel.: (679) 3314-466; Fax: (679) 3308-685 E-mail: usembsuva@is.com.fj *Mr. Frankie A. Reed, Ambassador*	c/o U.S. Embassy, Suva 31 Loftus Street, P.O. Box 218, Suva Fiji Tel.: (679) 3314-466; Fax: (679) 3308-685 *Michael Via, Economics Officer (E-mail: ViaMA@state.gov)*
Turkmenistan	U.S. Embassy No. 9 Pushkin Street Ashgabat, Turkmenistan 744000 Tel.: (99312) 350-045; Fax: (99312) 392-614 *Robert E. Patterson, Jr., Ambassador*	c/o U.S. Embassy Ashgabat 9 Pushkin St., Ashgabat 744000, Turkmenistan Tel.: (99312) 350-045; Fax: (99312) 392-614 *Mr.Trevor Boyd, Political/ Economic Officer* E-mail: BoydTW@state.gov
Tuvalu	c/o U.S. Embassy 31 Loftus Street Suva, Fiji Tel.: (679) 3314-466; Fax: (679) 3308-685 E-mail: usembsuva@is.com.fj *Mr. Frankie A. Reed, Ambassador*	c/o U.S. Embassy, Suva 31 Loftus Street, P.O. Box 218, Suva Fiji Tel.: (679) 3314-466; Fax: (679) 3308-685 Michael Via, Economics Officer (E-mail: ViaMA@state.gov)
Uzbekistan	U.S. Embassy 3 Moyqorghon Street, 5th Block, Yunusobod District, 100093 Tashkent, Uzbekistan Tel.: (998-71) 120-5450; Fax: (998-71) 120-6335 *George A. Krol, Ambassador*	c/o U.S. Embassy - Economic Section 41 Buyuk Turon Street, Sharq Building Tashkent, 700000 Uzbekistan Tel.: (998-71) 120-5450; Fax: (998-71) 120-6335 *William Laitinen, Political/Economic Officer* E-mail: laitinenwh@state.gov *Murod Madjidov, Economic Specialist* E-mail: MadjidovM@state.gov
Vanuatu	U.S. Embassy Douglas Street, Port Moresby Papua New Guinea P.O. Box 1492 Port Moresby NCD, Papua New Guinea Tel.: (675) 321-1455; Fax: (675) 320-0637 *Teddy B. Taylor, Ambassador* E-mail: png@state.gov	Commercial Section c/o U.S. Embassy, Port Moresby P.O. Box 1492 Port Moresby NCD, Papua New Guinea Tel.: (675) 321-1455 ext. 2136 Fax: (675)320-0637 *Mr. Regis Prevot, Economic/Political Officer* E-mail: PrevotRE@state.gov
Vietnam *Hanoi*	7 Lang Ha, Hanoi, Vietnam Tel.: (84-4) 3850-5000; Fax: (84-4) 3850-5010 *David B. Shear, Ambassador*	American Embassy US Commercial Service Rose GardenTower 170 Ngoc Khanh Street, Hanoi, Vietnam Tel.: (84-4) 3850-5199; Fax: (84-4) 3850-5064 *Yasue Pai, Commercial Officer* E-mail: Yasue.Pai@trade.gov *Ms. Tuyet Trees, Commercial Specialist* E-mail: Tuyet.Trees@trade.gov

COUNTRY	EMBASSY POST	COMMERCIAL POST
Vietnam *Ho Chi Minh City*	4 Le Duan Blvd., District 1 Ho Chi Minh City, Vietnam Tel.: (84-8) 3520-4200; Fax: (84-8) 3520-4244 *An T. Le, Consul General*	U.S. Commercial Service Diamond Plaza, 8F, 34 Le Duan Street, District 1 Ho Chi Minh City, Vietnam Tel.: (84-8) 825-0490; Fax: (84-8) 825-0491 *Mr. Patrick Wall, Senior Commercial Officer* E-mail: Patrick.Wall@trade.gov *Mr. My Tran, Commercial Specialist* E-mail: My.Tran@trade.gov

MULTILATERAL DEVELOPMENT BANKS	ADDRESS	COMMERCIAL POST
Asian Development Bank	Asian Development Bank 6 ADB Avenue, Mandaluyong City Metro Manila 0401, Philippines Tel.: (63-2) 632-4444 ext. 6051 Fax: (63-2) 632-4003; 632-2084 Website: www.adb.org *Amb. Robert Orr, U.S. Executive Director*	U.S. Commercial Service Liaison Office to the ADB U.S. Embassy –NOX 2 1201 Roxas Boulevard Ermita, Manila 1000 Philippines Tel.: (63-2) 516 5093; Fax: (63-2) 516 6958 *Ms. Margaret Keshishian, Senior Commercial Officer* E-mail: Margaret.Keshishian@trade.gov

Submitting Expressions of Interest

Consultant selection for technical assistance grants are based on the consultant's prior Expression of Interest (EOI). A good EOI should reflect the firm's experience and expertise in relation to the ADB project being pursued. It is important for a U.S. firm to emphasize this, or similar project experience in the country or in a similar geographic area rather than state a general profile of its consulting activities. When submitting an EOI, the project name should exactly match the one listed in this report to avoid confusion. Each project requires a separate EOI.

An EOI should be submitted on-line through the ADB website at www.adb.org. Firms may send a hardcopy follow-up to the Director, Central Operations Services 1 Division or to the Director, Central Operations Services 2 Division, with a copy to the ADB Project Officer.

Registering Consulting Firms and/or Individual Consultants

The ADB consultants registration system has been revised into a new and integrated system called **Consultant Management System (CMS)** for both consulting firms and individuals.

Records should be updated at least once a year; otherwise, inactive profiles will be de-activated and excluded from consultants' searches.

Visit www.adb.org/Consulting/cms.asp for more information.

U.S. Commercial Service Liaison Office to the Asian Development Bank (CS ADB) and the U.S. Executive Directors to the ADB Office (USED)

U.S. firms are encouraged to keep in contact with the **U.S. Commercial Service Liaison Office to the Asian Development Bank (CS ADB)** especially when they decide to participate in ADB procurement activities. This office works closely with the Office of the U.S. Executive Director to the ADB (USED) to increase American awareness of, and participation in, the ADB's procurement activities.

For CS ADB assistance, please contact: Ms. Margaret Keshishian, Director (E-mail: Margaret.Keshishian@trade.gov)

U.S. firms may also notify their interest to pursue ADB business opportunities by sending a copy of their Expressions of Interest (EOI) to CS ADB to either of the following addresses:

U.S. mailing address:
> Attention: CS/ADB
> Unit 8600, Box 1565
> DPO AP 96515-1565,

or international mailing address:

> U.S. Embassy – NOX 2
> 1201 Roxas Boulevard,
> Ermita, Manila 1000
> Philippines
> Phone: (63-2) 516 5093; Fax: (63-2) 516 6958
> E-mail: Office.ManilaADB@trade.gov

For More Information

The U.S. Commercial Service Liaison Office to the Asian Development Bank, located in Makati City, Philippines can be contacted via e-mail at: Office.ManilaADB@trade.gov; Phone: 632 887-1345; Fax: 632 887-1164; or visit our website: http://export.gov/adb

The U.S. Commercial Service — Your Global Business Partner

With its network of offices across the United States and in more than 80 countries, the U.S. Commercial Service of the U.S. Department of Commerce utilizes its global presence and international marketing expertise to help U.S. companies sell their products and services worldwide. Locate the U.S. Commercial Service trade specialist in the U.S. nearest you by visiting **http://www.export.gov/eac**.

Comments and Suggestions: We welcome your comments and suggestions regarding this market research. You can e-mail us your comments/suggestions to: **Customer.Care@mail.doc.gov**. Please include the name of the applicable market research in your e-mail. We greatly appreciate your feedback.